OUT OF LONDON WALKS

Great Escapes by Britain's Best
Walking Tour Company

2 4 6 8 10 9 7 5 3 1

First published in the UK in 2012 by Virgin Books,
an imprint of Ebury Publishing
A Random House Group Company
Copyright © David Tucker and the contributors as identified
in the Work 2012

General Editor: Stephen Barnett
Drawings © Pete Scully
Maps © Nick Turzynski
Photography inset section: p 1 © Brian Burnell; p 2 (bottom) © Chris Metcalfe;
p 3 (top and bottom) © Mark Steele; p 4 (top) © John Blakey (bottom) © Dave Ball;
p 5 © Ursula Haigh; p 6 (top) © Paulo Saldanha (bottom) © James Harvey;
p 7 (top) © David Iliff/licensed via Wikimedia Commons Licence CC-BY-SA 3.0;
p 8 © John Starnes

www.randomhouse.co.uk

Addresses for companies within The Random House Group Limited
can be found at www.randomhouse.co.uk/offices.htm

The Random House Group Limited Reg. No. 954009

A CIP catalogue record for this book is available from the British Library

Design and typeset by K.DESIGN, Winscombe, Somerset

ISBN: 9780753540572

To buy books by your favourite authors and register for offers, visit
www.randomhouse.co.uk

Printed and bound in Great Britain by Clays Ltd, St Ives PLC

Dedicated, with respect and admiration,
to the modern Marco Polos: to all of you – the tolerant,
curious, companionable, bright, determined, durable,
friendly, funny, switched-on, and ever-gallant
London Walkers and London Walks Day Trippers.

Contents

INTRODUCTION

DAVID TUCKER

'Always drink upstream from the herd.'
WILL ROGERS

Get out more. Get out of London. Get out and walk. Get out of the coach. Get out of the motorway rut. Get out of the tourism equivalent of factory farming.

OK, some background. London Walks does out-of-town trips? We most certainly do. And they're cut from the same cloth as our walking tours in London – even unto their genesis.

In the beginning, an Australian named Keith Baverstock – one of life's difference makers* – founded London Walks. That was half a century ago. Keith was

---

* That's no exaggeration. Keith also started white-water rafting on the driest continent on Earth – and 'Colonial Day Simulacra' in Australian schools.

fed up with the banality of typical London tourist fare, so he started what is now the oldest urban walking-tour company in the world, the gold standard of urban walking-tour companies.

Fast forward to 1990. Mary and I have just inherited London Walks (from Ian, the guide who took up the reins when Keith went back to Australia in 1973). Our first draft pick (as they say in the NFL) for a guide to join us was a gifted actor named Richard Bartlett. Richard was a natural: the honeyed voice, warmth, urbanity, presence, perfect timing, wit, connections to die for – the fit was perfect.

One of the curious things about this craft of ours is that real guiding – London Walks guiding (as opposed to parrot patter) – is something you come to quite a bit later in life. No eight-year-old (or twenty-year-old for that matter) ever thinks, 'I want to be a guide when I grow up.' Footballer or fireman or doctor or dancer or actor or author, yes. But not a guide. It's something you find – or it finds you – when you're grown-up, and when the day does finally dawn, it's a road-to-Damascus moment, for the really gifted ones at any rate. It may have taken half a lifetime, but you've found what you were put on Earth to do. To paraphrase Yeats's great line, who can separate the guide from the guiding?

In Richard's case, that meant, among other things, that he was on to the Blue Badge Guide course almost as soon as he got the bit between his teeth. 'What? There are places I'm not allowed to guide? [You have to be a Blue Badge Guide to guide in Westminster Abbey, for example.] I'm not having that.' So, yes, straight on to the course. And straight through it. It's a two-year course. Richard aced it in one.

Now to come to the Genesis Part II point. *The Blue Badge course is by no means a London only matter.* Oxford, Canterbury, Windsor, Stonehenge, and plenty of other places are also part of its syllabus, part of its remit. For a London-based guide that meant (notice the tense) coach excursion guiding: any number – industrial, mass-production numbers – of coach loads of tourists, 'moleing' (crawl-stop, crawl-stop, crawl-stop) through London rush-hour traffic and then grinding out the motorway miles on day tours that 'package' (the *mot juste*) inevitably superficial, get-out-and-stretch-a-leg 'visits' to three, four, or even five destinations. It's transformative, that. Oxford, Bath, Canterbury and the others are Rembrandts or Constables. 'Doing them' that way turns Old Masters into paint-by-numbers. 'There has to be a better way of doing it,' was Richard's thought.

The better way was, of course, the London Walks way – walking tours. And once you're thinking walking tours in Bath or Canterbury or Oxford, well, everything follows from that.

We had to slip the surly bonds of the coach. The coach was the prison house. Get shot of it. It was what was locking up the time we needed to do full-blooded walking tours that would do justice to the places we were visiting. We wanted to convey a real feel for these places – their history, their byways and hidden bits and bobs, their inscapes, what makes them tick, what it was (and is) like to live there – as opposed to a postcard glimpse.

And *voilà*, there it was. Ours for the, er, taking. Trains. Much faster. Much more comfortable. 'Fastly superior'.

OK, we *do* use coaches – sparingly, shrewdly, locally. One of our Cambridge outings is a perfect case in point. With the flexibility the coach gives him, our guide Simon is able to take his party out to the village of Madingley, three miles west of Cambridge, to see the very beautiful and moving Cambridge-American Cemetery and Memorial. The cemetery is the final resting place of some 3,000 Second World War US airmen. It's a corner of England where, on the wings of beauty and quiescence and a few unerring words – 'To you from failing hands we throw the torch – be yours to hold it high' – you really do sense 'a presence far more deeply interfused'.

Interfused is a note you can sound again. Interfusing is what a great guide does. In this instance, it's Simon stacking interest by fashioning a route out to Madingley that takes us through the outskirts of Cambridge, an area that is 'renowned but unvisited' – scientific Cambridge. Here is where the Cavendish Labs are located, and the British Antarctica Survey has its headquarters, among many other world-famous institutions.

But beyond the *modus operandi*, the fundamental of fundamentals: *it all comes down to the guiding.* You get the very best guides and let them get on with it. What that means – be it out on the street or here on the page – is an individual, guide-created ascent,* something that's personal, richly particular, unfailingly intelligent and finely wrought, and that draws together. That's what the great ones can do. They can fashion a route that's full of interest and surprises. They can find – or make – the

---

*The mountaineering metaphor isn't too much of a stretch. Guides of this calibre are operating at a different level entirely; theirs are the names up on the leaderboards of peer-reviewed assessments and eminent travel publications. (For example, *Travel & Leisure* recently naming Karen one of 'the world's [15] greatest guides'.)

11

connections that galvanise all those brightly coloured bits into a mosaic, providing shape and coherence. Without meaning of that sort, you've just got a jumble sale of a tour. The guide is the linchpin. Our guides can serve up tours in a way that takes their walkers with them and holds, even grips, them for two hours.

Of course, certain keys go some way towards accounting for the magic – local knowledge for starters. Alison lives in St Albans. Nick wrote his chapter on Stratford-upon-Avon towards the end of the year that he spent there with the Royal Shakespeare Company. Richard has a country house in Suffolk (one of the trips that, alas, didn't make it into the book). Local knowledge is something that all the London Walks guides have. They don't do off-the-peg guiding. They've drilled down much deeper. They've become a part of the places they talk about. And they've earned the trust of the locals. That, in turn, opens up magic casement after magic casement.

Great English guides, great English places. You should all have the great good fortune to spend a day with them in the places they 'curate' – with Richard in Oxford, or Hilary in Winchester, or Chris in Hampton Court, or Gillian in Chartwell, or Karen in Bath. Which, come to think of it, makes this little book the magic carpet. Because now you can.

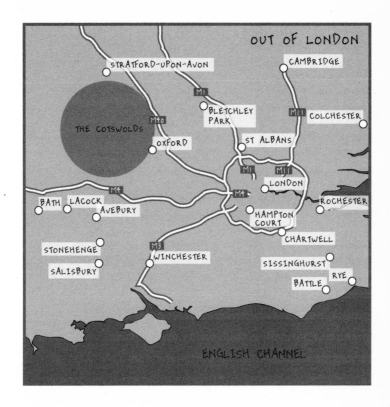

CAMBRIDGE – GOLDEN WILLOWS BY THE RIVERSIDE

SIMON LAW

Cambridge looks down on Oxford, calling it 'the Other Place'. Never mention the O word in Cambridge. 'But,' says the Other Place, 'Lewis Carroll, J.R.R. Tolkien, Margaret Thatcher, Tony Blair, Bill Clinton, Hugh Grant ...'

'Really?' says Cambridge. 'Newton, Darwin.' Surnames suffice ... which, you might think, says everything. Well, not quite. There is also Trinity College, which has produced more than thirty Nobel Prize winners (more than most countries!); the cracking of the DNA code; the discovery of the electron and the neutron; the man whose team first split the atom; the discoverer of blood circulation; the inventor of the jet engine; and computing and those who made it possible – Babbage, Wilkes and Turing.

The traditions, beauty and architecture of Cambridge have inspired great poets and writers. It has the most remarkable Gothic building in the world – the Chapel of King's College, which E.M. Forster, a King's alumnus, described as 'an incomparable building. There is nothing like it in the world. It triumphs through three mediums: stone, glass, wood ... One has no doubts as to its greatness. It is one of the great buildings of the world and it is unique. If it perished, no millionaire and no government could replace it.'

Simply standing and viewing the building across the velvet lawn from the 'Backs', where the River Cam flows, is stunning. Better still, see it from the river itself by gliding along on a punt – the flat-bottomed craft Cambridge has made its own – as the poet Rupert Brooke so often did as a young man a century ago: 'I only know that you may lie / All day and watch the Cambridge sky.' Then to enter the chapel is literally (for I have often heard it happen) breathtaking.

In 1448 the college's founder, that most spiritual of kings, Henry VI, decreed that the chapel 'shall contain in length 288 feet of assize without any Aisles and all of the wideness of 40 feet, being in height 90ft, embattled, vaulted ... sufficiently buttressed and every buttress fined with finials (pinnacles).'

His studiousness and faith in God proved to be inadequate shields against the powerful schemers of late medieval England. Hapless Henry was captured by his murderous cousin Edward during the dynastic Wars of the Roses. He never saw his plans completed. His eventual successor, that most pedantic of kings, Henry VII, bequeathed £5000 in gold: 'that thereby should not be only a notable act and a meritorious work perfected, which else were like to grow to desolation and never to have been done and accomplished, but also divine service

17

and hereafter maintained and supported to the honour and laud of Almighty God.'

The wooden payment chest is still there in the chapel for all to see. The gold was all well spent on what novelist Henry James described as master mason John Wastell's 'sublime creation': the chapel's vaulted ceiling. '[It has] such a beautiful slimness of clustered tracery soaring along the walls and spreading, bending and commingling in the roof, that its simplicity seems only a richness the more.'

Poet Samuel Taylor Coleridge went further: 'the marvellous sublimity and transcendent beauty is quite unparalleled.' This beauty, more than 1800 tons of beauty, supports itself, making the ceiling an architectural wonder of the world. It would be another two centuries before Cambridge gave birth to Newtonian physics. The masons of Gothic architecture were students of trial and error. Experience and intuition counted for all. In 1762, Horace Walpole described the reaction of England's greatest architect, Sir Christopher Wren, when he surveyed the building: 'Wren ... said that if any man would show him where to put the first stone, he would engage to build such another.'

The second Henry Tudor we remember largely for his powers of destruction. Monks, Roman Catholicism, pilgrimages, his wives' heads – all of these he removed from English life. Yet without his plundering of the monasteries and his Machiavellian act of generosity towards Cambridge – he effectively bribed the university to secure their support for his divorce from his first wife, Catherine of Aragon – then Cambridge would never have been endowed with the best example of Renaissance stained-glass window work in the world with its brilliant rainbow of biblical scenes. The tales depicted are from the Old and New Testaments but the faces and clothes are of sixteenth-century England. Henry himself appears, his face attached to the persona of King Solomon, who receives gifts from the Queen of Sheba. Was that the artists' cheeky prank? Or their flattering of the fearful, forty-inch-chest reginacide?

The huge east window at the chapel's far end is the most impressive, depicting Christ's trial, suffering through crucifixion, death and deposition from the cross. The window's six scenes are peppered with pained, ecstatic and hauntingly grotesque faces, something akin to those of Brueghel, yet their innate luminosity renders them more vivid and entrancing.

It took more than thirty years for the finest glaziers from London, Flanders and Germany to create their masterpieces with 'goode clean sure and perfect glass and orient colours and imagery the story of the old law and the new law' (as their contract of 1526 stated). 'In blazing glass above the dark / Glow skies and thrones and wings / Blue, ruby, gold and green / Between the whiteness of the walls' wrote Poet Laureate John Betjeman after the Second World War.

On 1 September 1939, when the Wehrmacht first engaged Polish forces, telegrams were sent to arrange for removal of the stained glass. By the time the Imperial Japanese Army were ravaging Hong Kong more than two years later, all the glass – thousands of jewel-like pieces – had been stored in Cambridge cellars to protect it from any air raids. Twenty-eight people were killed by falling bombs in Cambridge but, compared with other similar-sized cities, Cambridge survived relatively unharmed. Adolf Hitler, it was claimed, had bought a house a few miles down the road in Huntingdon before the war and the SS had already earmarked St John's College for use as a regional HQ following Operation Sealion, Hitler's planned invasion of Britain. The preponderance of eagles decorating gateposts and buildings at John's must have struck a chord with perceptions of Teutonic destiny.

Only two great medieval English churches retain their stained glass in anything approaching its original state and King's Chapel is one (the other is York Minster). During the Civil War, much was destroyed by parliamentary soldiers, who perceived such ecclesiastical decoration as popish. The King's Chapel windows are thought to have been saved by virtue of the harsh seventeenth-century Cambridge winter climate. Roundhead soldiers were quartered in the chapel and smashing the windows would have led to freezing-cold, sleepless nights.

As visitors exit the chapel, many have their eyes drawn to the lawn between them and the river. The 'Keep off the Grass' sign ensures the patch remains pristine. Indeed, only the colleges' senior members, or fellows, may defy such notices! Pink Floyd lyricist Roger Waters claimed that this prohibition prompted him to write the words 'The lunatic is on the grass' in his song 'Brain damage' on the album 'Dark Side of the Moon'. He and his Cambridge schoolfriend Syd Barrett, whose descent into drug-induced lunacy inspired the song, performed for students and locals during the band's early days.

Music is a strong element in Cambridge's make-up. Choirs abound and King's College's is of world renown. The BBC broadcasts its 'Festival of Nine Lessons and Carols' from King's each Christmas Eve at 3 p.m. People queue from five in the morning to attend.

Next to the chapel stands the Gibbs building, wherein economist J.M. Keynes had his desk. It is haunted by another Barrett, a former fellow whose room contained a coffin. Some attributed Barrett's strange habits and manner to his flirtation with diabolic forces of evil. One fateful night, Barrett's screams were heard echoing down the hall. When the door of his room was opened the next day, Barrett was discovered dead in his coffin. His late-night ghostly screams may be heard each year on the anniversary of his death.

Fittingly, M.R. James, who penned some of the greatest ghost stories in English literature, studied at King's in the 1880s and eventually became the college head, or Master. Indeed, Cambridge is one of the most haunted cities in Britain – unsurprising for a city suffused in at least eight centuries of intense mental and spiritual energy.

Cambridge has more than thirty colleges. They provide students with accommodation, a dining hall, a chapel and small library. The fellows may relax in the combination room. The oldest college is Peterhouse, founded in 1284. A white figure haunts the hall and combination room, which are joined by a passageway that passes through a fifteenth-century bell tower. One explanation – that the ghost is that of James Davies, a fellow who hanged himself at the college in 1789 – seemed unlikely as Davies's obituary stated that his suicide occurred in the chapel. However, in 1998, in college records, his coffin bill was discovered, which stated that his body had been found hanging in the bell tower!

Students at Sidney Sussex College have witnessed the appearance of a floating, yellowish human head accompanied by the smell of rotting human flesh. The most famous Sidney alumnus is Oliver Cromwell, parliamentary commander in the Civil War against Charles I. Cromwell studied there for just one year, arriving in 1616 on the day that Shakespeare died. In 1649, Cromwell's signature was one of many on Charles's death warrant, following the king's defeat. Cromwell subsequently ruled England as 'Lord Protector' but died in 1658 and was buried in Westminster Abbey. The dead king's son, Charles II, returned from exile and took revenge. Cromwell's body was dug up, put on trial, sentenced to death, hanged and beheaded. His head was set on a spike on the roof of Westminster Hall but, after more than twenty years, blew off in a storm and was conveyed to a museum. Over the following decades, it was sold on from one owner to the next until finally it was presented to Sidney Sussex where it was buried in 1960, somewhere near the ante-chapel. Only three people are said to know its secret location.

Although no metropolis, Cambridge has some of the finest small museums in the land. Now open to the public, many of these museums had their beginnings in academic purposes. The Fitzwilliam is said to be the best outside London. Thomas Lethbridge, twentieth-century curator of the archaeological museum, claimed it was haunted and that an ancient skull would move from cabinet to cabinet. His passion for paranormal, occult and extraterrestrial matters led to academic ostracism.

Just around the corner is the zoology museum, its shelves stacked with specimens labelled 'CHARLES DARWIN. BEAGLE VOYAGE.' When Darwin arrived at Cambridge University, today's Zoology site contained the University Botanical Gardens – subsequently relocated – where Darwin and John Henslow (botany professor) would regularly stroll together.

Although young Charles was originally destined for a church career, he had an open enquiring mind when it came to the newly emerging sciences, and Henslow held regular Friday evening soirees where like-minded staff and students could mingle. Darwin later recalled: 'At these parties I have listened to the great men of those days, conversing on all sorts of subjects with the most varied and brilliant powers.' He even began attending Henslow's botany lectures, noting: 'His strongest taste was to draw conclusions from his long-continued minute observations.' One of Darwin's fellow students later recounted: 'The professor ... said he hoped his teaching influenced many to perseverance – certainly he knew it had influenced one – no doubt he meant Darwin.'

Through Henslow, Darwin was introduced to geology professor Adam Sedgwick, and fossil collecting soon became a hobby. After one lecture, Darwin commented on Sedgwick's 'enlarged views of both time and space' and his 'drawing large cheques upon the Bank of Time'. The importance of these two great Cambridge professors in shaping Darwin's theory of evolution, which he put forward in his 1859 publication *On the Origin of Species*, is clearly discernible.

The New Museums site is adorned with memorials commemorating world-changing discoveries and the personalities involved, such as Crick, Watson and Rutherford, who along with nearly thirty Nobel Prize winners worked at the Cavendish Laboratory – the nation's first research laboratory for physical sciences. All departments of the Cavendish relocated westwards in 1974 to a new site where the new disciplines of nanotechnology and computer science further Cambridge's reputation as a world leader in science with more Nobel prizes to date than any university on earth.

Opposite the old Cavendish gateway sits Corpus Christi College, where they still have a contemporary portrait of Christopher Marlowe, who gained a Master's Degree there. An Elizabethan spy, assassinated in a London pub, Marlowe was a highly imaginative playwright and is claimed by some to have been the true author of Shakespeare's plays.

Corpus Christi's library is a real treasure chest. Many of the thirteenth-century college's original works were lost when rioting peasants ran amok in the famous revolt in 1381, but in 1574 Archbishop Matthew Parker bequeathed more books and manuscripts to his *alma mater*. As archbishop, the large-nosed Parker earned a reputation for making excessive enquiries into the activities of his clergymen – the original 'nosey parker'!

College records reveal that as a student Parker borrowed two valuable books, which he neglected to return. Parker later developed the practice on a much grander scale. He became Anne Boleyn's chaplain. She made him dean of Stoke-by-Clare College. Their library collection shrank as Parker's grew. His later appointment as Archbishop of Canterbury really enabled him to indulge his appetite for acquisition. Parker plundered the libraries of monasteries that Henry VIII had dissolved, but in so doing preserved national treasures that might otherwise have been lost.

Keen to justify Henry VIII's break from Roman Catholicism, Parker sought evidence for the precedent of an independent English church in ancient Anglo-Saxon texts. Thus, today in the college's Parker Library can be found original works by the Venerable Bede and King Alfred the Great; the oldest version of the Anglo Saxon Chronicle, which Alfred himself ordered to be written; the gospels brought to England by St Augustine in AD 597 (one of the oldest books in the world), and many more of note. Parker's gift to the library numbered around one and a half thousand books and manuscripts, but it came with a condition – should books go missing (how ironic!) Corpus would forfeit the collection to Gonville and Caius college and they to Trinity Hall. The rule also applied to Parker's silver collection. Hence, every autumn, a ceremonial audit involving the three colleges' representatives takes place. No books or silverware have yet disappeared – in more than 400 years! So hats off to Matthew Parker, although the old adage, 'set a thief to catch a thief', is brought to mind.

Every college has a library but Trinity's is surely the most elegant. Its architect, Sir Christopher Wren, even designed the shelves and furniture. Wren made optimum use of space and light with, for a library, unprecedentedly large windows, constructed above the gorgeous limewood shelves that have carvings by Grinling Gibbons, England's greatest ever woodcarver. The sculptor Louis Francois Roubiliac executed the marble busts of college alumni. This late seventeenth-century triumph of wood, glass and stone reflects the age that created it as much as King's Chapel. Wren, professor of mathematics at (regrettably) the Other Place, was a friend of Isaac Barrow, professor of mathematics at Cambridge, who was a close friend of Sir Isaac Newton's. Barrow recognised Newton's genius and therefore resigned his post to accommodate the better man.

Encased and on display in the library is *Principia Mathematica*, Newton's work outlining the laws of gravity and motion in space. (Nearby lies the original manuscript of A.A. Milne's *Winnie the Pooh*. Milne and his son, Christopher Robin, were both Trinity men.) The library overlooks a courtyard, Nevile's Court, where Newton calculated the speed of sound by kicking against the wall and timing the echo. In April 1705, Queen Anne arrived at Trinity College to knight him. Newton's statue dominates the ante-chapel of Trinity's chapel (Roubiliac again). Poet William Wordsworth, who studied next door at St John's College, recalled in his *Prelude* of 1799 how

> From my pillow looking forth by light
> Of moon or favouring stars, I could behold
> The Antechapel where the statue stood
> Of Newton with his prism and silent face,
> The marble index of a mind forever
> Voyaging through strange seas of thought alone.

In his autobiographical work, Wordsworth also recalls the clock tower of Trinity's Great Court with its 'male and female voice' – one high and low note for each hour struck. Twelve o'clock (24 dings and dongs) takes 43 seconds to strike. The court's circumference is 400 yards. For decades, at noon, students have tried to run the distance before the chimes stop. This tradition was immortalised in the film *Chariots of Fire*.

The chimes of another Cambridge clock tower – that of the church of St Mary the Great – are, inadvertently, the most famous in the world. St Mary's is the university church where, at one time, degrees were awarded. In 1834, the old Palace of Westminster in London was destroyed by fire. A new palace was created there with an enormous clock tower containing a large hour bell called Big Ben. Discussions arose about the choice of tune for the chimes to herald Big Ben. One member of the committee was a Cambridge man and suggested that the tune of his university church should be adopted. It was. So now, Cambridge chimes (not Westminster chimes) are famous throughout the world.

Behind the church is the daily market. Cambridge has been a market town since Saxon times. For centuries, fresh fish was brought in from the coast along the River Cam. Until 1914 the market sold 'Cambridge butter' in yard-long rolls of 1 inch diameter. Although the tradition has died, university officials still carry iron measuring rods in ceremonial processions. Their predecessors once used these rods to ensure the honesty of dairy traders in days when the university had enormous powers over the townspeople's livelihoods.

Rivalry between 'town' and 'gown' often descended into physical violence. Indeed, it is said that the university's foundation more than eight centuries ago resulted from terrified students fleeing to Cambridge from lynching in the Other Place. Today, however, around 18,000 university students mix happily with shoppers drawn by the town's impressive array of retail opportunities, pubs and cafés, and with visitors who come for more ... and more. So. Much. More. This one chapter is merely toe-dipping in the Cam. Visitors always need to return.

In the 1920s, Chinese poet Hsu Chih Mo studied at King's and in 2008 the college placed a marble stone near the banks of the Cam inscribed with lines in Mandarin from his poem, 'Saying Goodbye to Cambridge Again'. Largely unheard of in the West, the poem is known and recited by millions of Chinese, including tourists and postgraduates who have come to Cambridge in recent years to follow in the poet's footsteps. The poem includes the following lines:

Very quietly I take my leave
As quietly as I came here ...
The golden willows by the riverside ...
Their reflections on the shimmering waves
Always linger in the depth of my heart.

Oxford and the Cotswolds – those dreaming spires

RICHARD BARTLETT

B egin your walk in Oxford in Broad Street, outside the famous Blackwells bookstore and across the road from the thirteen 'emperors' heads, busts originally commissioned in the seventeenth century and replaced twice since then. The building to the right of the heads, with the green shield above the door, is also of this period and was home to the original Ashmolean Museum. The first purpose-built museum in the world, this housed the collection of antiquities that Elias Ashmole, who had received a doctorate in medicine from Oxford, had donated to the university. Many more artefacts were acquired over the following years, forcing a move to larger premises in Beaumont Street in the mid-nineteenth century. Today, the original building houses the Museum of the History of Science.

Cross the road and walk through the small gate between the row of emperors' heads, turning to your right. Facing you is the north front of the Divinity School, the first dedicated building of the university, dating from the mid 1400s. The university's origins go back to the 1100s when it was established as a place of learning after Henry II had banned English students from attending the university in Paris. In the early days of the university, frequent conflicts broke out between 'town and gown', the townspeople and the university students. After one riot – during which a group of students had to flee for their lives and subsequently started a university in Cambridge – the university here decided that it would be best for the students to live with the masters, and hall houses were established. By the middle of the 1200s, this went a step further with the founding of three colleges within the university – University, Merton and Balliol. These were endowed houses, presided over by a master, providing bedrooms, a dining hall, chapel and library. The teaching was done by the university.

Note the wonderful amount of glass in the Divinity School. At one time this included beautiful stained-glass windows, telling the story of the Bible, but sadly these were destroyed in the seventeenth century, after the Civil War. In this building, not only were students taught but exams, called disputations, were conducted. The students would enter the hall in pairs and stand in what looked like wooden pulpits. The examiners, sitting in the body of the hall, asked questions of the students and then gave them a subject to debate. All subjects read at Oxford had these oral exams until the early nineteenth century when it was becoming apparent that the richer students always seemed to achieve a degree (possibly by bribing the examiners?) and so written exams were introduced.

Opposite the Divinity School is the Sheldonian Theatre. In the seventeenth century, the university decided it needed a building for academic celebrations and for the regular meetings of Congregation, the body of resident Masters of Arts that controls university affairs. The university approached Gilbert Sheldon, Warden of All Souls College and, later, Archbishop of Canterbury, who was persuaded to donate the money for the building. The architect chosen to design the theatre was a young man already here at the university, Christopher Wren. The Sheldonian, along with the chapel of Pembroke College, Cambridge, were Wren's first major commissions. Today, the theatre hosts the ceremony of matriculation, where students are made members of the university and a few years later, they hope, return to receive their degrees.

Walking between these buildings, you will find an open space with the grand Clarendon building on your left. This was designed by Nicholas Hawksmoor, a pupil of Christopher Wren's, in the early eighteenth century to house the university's printing presses. Today, the University Press is based outside the city and the Clarendon building has been taken over by the admissions department of the university library.

Turning to your right and proceeding through the archway behind you brings you to Old Schools Quad. To the right is the Proscholium, now the entrance to the Divinity School and to the Bodleian Library. In the early seventeenth century, Thomas Bodley offered to fund a new library for the university, and he made an agreement with the Stationer's Company of London to put a copy of every book registered with them in this library. The three wings that surround you were built to house them all.

At the east end of the quadrangle is the Tower of the Five Orders. This is the largest gate tower in England and so named for the five orders of classic architecture represented in the columns – Tuscan, Doric, Ionic, Corinthian and Composite. On the ground floor of the quadrangle buildings can be seen the entrances to the lecture rooms with their Latin inscriptions above. As the library's collections expanded, these rooms were gradually taken over.

Leaving the quadrangle by the arch to the south, you will see rising before you the glorious circular Radcliffe Camera. The money for the building came from John Radcliffe, physician to William III and Mary II, and he also provided an endowment with which to purchase books. The Radcliffe was the first circular library in England, and although originally it had a varied collection of books, it became known for its science holding. Today, the library collections have moved to other premises and the building is a reading room for the Bodleian Library.

Keeping the Radcliffe to the right, a few steps further on brings you to St Mary's church, known as the university church. The original church that stood here was adopted in the late twelfth century by the university, and became the seat of the university's government. It was also used for lectures and the awarding of degrees. The church was mostly rebuilt in the fifteenth century; the oldest part of it today is the fourteenth-century tower and spire, the spire being one of the earliest examples of Gothic architecture in England.

To your left are the gates of All Souls College, which was founded in the mid-fifteenth century and is now one of the great research colleges. The unusual towers on the far side of the quadrangle were built in the early eighteenth century. Walk past the church, keeping it to your right, and you now cross High Street. On your right is the Carfax tower, all that remains of a thirteenth-century church. It was here, where the four main streets of the city crossed, that the town's market grew up. By the eighteenth century it had become too big for its original site and was moved to the now famous covered market, on the right. The tower, at 23 metres (75½ feet), is the tallest building in the centre of Oxford, and no other buildings may be erected taller than this. If you have the energy, walk to the top of the tower; from the viewing gallery you get the most wonderful views of the city. Oxford was called the 'city of dreaming spires' by poet Matthew Arnold, and from here you can see why.

Meanwhile, back at ground level, the nearby statue honours Cecil Rhodes and is part of Oriel College, where Rhodes was a student. His famous Rhodes scholarships were funded from part of the vast fortune he later acquired in southern Africa.

Keeping the statue to your left, walk up High Street and take the first turning to your left. On your left is part of Oriel College and to your right a number of brightly coloured houses where some of the students live. You now enter Oriel Square and can see the main entrance to the college. Have a peep through the open wooden doors into the quadrangle. Although the college was founded in the fourteenth century, most of the buildings you see are from the seventeenth century. On the far side of the quadrangle, above the entrance to the dining hall, are two statues. One is of Edward II, in whose reign the college was opened, and to his left, Charles I. Above them is a statue of the Virgin Mary in whose name the college was originally founded.

Carry on your walk, stopping at the next corner. On your right is one of the entrances to Christ Church College, which was founded by Henry VIII in the sixteenth century. In front of you and to your left, on the opposite side of the road, is Corpus Christi College (1517). If you are here in the afternoon, this college will often be open and, if so, enter through the main gates and walk into the quadrangle. This is one of the rare examples of a paved quadrangle. In most colleges, you will find that they are grassed. In the centre of the quadrangle is the pillar sundial, known as the Pelican Sundial.

On the far side of the quad to your right is an archway. Go through here and you will soon be in the most beautiful garden. Keep walking until you are standing in front of a low wall. Below are the immaculate gardens of Christ Church College. You will see the college buildings to your right, including their chapel, which is the cathedral of Oxford. The bustle of the city is just a few moments away but here you look out on to tranquil meadows, where cattle often graze. Originally, all colleges had to be built within the city walls and the effect is that the city has not encroached on the surrounding countryside. In the distance, a line of trees marks the river. In the summer, you can see and hear the students cheering on their college teams in boat races.

Now retrace your steps, return to the road and turn right. This will give you an idea of how Oxford would have looked around the sixteenth century. Little has changed, and even the road is still cobbled. On your right is Merton College and on your left University College, two of the original colleges, founded in the thirteenth century. As the road turns to the left, the building you now see is the Examination Schools. Although seventeenth century (Jacobean) in style, it was actually built towards the end of the nineteenth century. It is the main lecture facility of the university.

Keep walking and you find yourself back in High Street. Cross over the road and turn left, taking the first road to your right. On your right is the entrance to St Edmund Hall; once again, go in if it's open and wander into the quadrangle. St Edmund was one of the early thirteenth-century halls that laid the foundation of the university. Most of the college was rebuilt in the seventeenth century but the left-hand side of the quadrangle gives an idea of how the original buildings might have looked – just two-storeyed with many small windows and low entrance doors.

To the far end of the quadrangle is the chapel, and over it the library. Behind you is the dining hall and in the middle of the quadrangle a medieval well. Go through the low arch on your left and you enter the gardens of the college. The gardens are also the graveyard of the twelfth-century church in front of you, St Peter-in-the-East. Originally, the fortified city of Oxford had four gates and by each gate a church was built. After the Second World War, the upkeep of the East Gate church proved too expensive and it was given to the college. As St Edmund already possessed an adequate chapel, they decided to deconsecrate the old church and use it to create a modern library. The seated statue to your left is St Edmund as a poor student.

Return now to the road and turn right following the narrow winding lane. To the right are the walls of Queen's College. Founded in the 1300s during the reign of Edward III, the college is named for his queen, Philippa of Hainault. The entire college was rebuilt, mostly in the baroque style, in the early eighteenth century. On your left, you come to the gates of our next college. The kneeling figure that can be seen up and to the right is of the man who founded the college in the early fourteenth century, William of Wykeham, Bishop of Winchester. The statue in the middle is the

Virgin Mary, and the original college was named The College of St Mary of Winchester in Oxford. As Oriel College was also dedicated to the Virgin Mary, this college became known as the New St Mary's College, and today as just New. Here you will have to pay to go in but it is well worth the entrance fee. The buildings on three sides of the quadrangle were just two storeys to start with, but a third was added in the 1600s. In the 1700s, all the windows were replaced with sash windows. If you look to the far side of the quadrangle, to the left of the first floor, you will see one of the original windows. Imagine the buildings in the original two-storey form and with such windows and you'll get an idea of what the quadrangle would have looked like 700 years ago.

Notice the tower with a fine staircase leading up into it in the far left corner, and the original buildings on the left side of the quadrangle. This is the hall and chapel. Turn left and go through the arch to enter the chapel. The glass surrounding you in the antechapel is medieval and original, with the exception of the west window, which is painted glass designed by Sir Joshua Reynolds. Below this is a remarkable statue by Sir Jacob Epstein, 'Lazarus breaking from the bounds'.

The chapel itself is one of the largest and most beautiful in all the colleges. The wooden stalls, where the choir and students sit, lead down on both sides to the high altar. Behind this is a magnificent stone reredos, filled with statues. To the right of the high altar is a portrait of Wykeham, carrying his crozier. This silver gilt crozier can still be seen in the glass-fronted case opposite. Beside this is a portrait by El Greco.

Look up to the extraordinary hammer-beamed ceiling, seemingly held up by the statues of the angels. The acoustics in the chapel make it much sought-after for music recording, and the choir has a worldwide reputation with one hundred recordings to its name. Leaving the chapel, turn to your left, walk to the opposite end of the quadrangle and climb the stone stairs into the dining hall. This is a breathtaking space with linenfold panelling. Refectory tables face the far end of the hall, where the high table is raised up by two steps, behind which is another picture of the founder and numerous other portraits of benefactors. In the middle of the lofty ceiling are louvred windows, where the smoke from the fire that once would have been lit in the middle of the hall escaped. Above you, at the opposite end of the hall – where you entered – is a musicians' gallery.

Now retrace your steps to the quadrangle, turning left then left again to bring you to the gardens. The wall you see to the left is the original fortified city wall, which

Wykeham had to buy and retain when he bought the land for his college. In front of it is the most glorious herbaceous border. The wrought-iron gates you walk through carry the motto of the college – 'Manners Makyth Man'.

Returning to the entrance to the college, carry on along the road in front of you. Does the bridge look familiar? Built last century, it is based upon the design of the Bridge of Sighs in Venice. Passing under this, and turning right then left, will bring you to where your walk began. If you have a little more time and would like to visit a number of other colleges, simply walk along Broad Street until you arrive at Turl Street, the first turning to your left. Down here you will find Exeter and Lincoln College on the left and Jesus College, founded by Elizabeth I, on your right.

* * *

North of Oxford lie the Cotswolds, one of the most beautiful areas of countryside in England. The undulating landscape with spectacular vistas, the field patterns, the drystone walls and hedgerows, copses of trees, and the charming little villages nestled in the valleys by the rivers conjure up an England of the past.

The name 'Cotswold' comes from two old English words – 'cot', a sheep's pen, and 'wold', a hill – and means sheep pens in the hills. Even before the Romans invaded Britain, the people of this area were rearing sheep. The Romans crossbred their own with the English varieties and produced a large animal with a long fleece that was ideal for hand spinning. After the Norman invasion of the eleventh century, much of the Cotswolds was given over to the nobles who had helped William the Conqueror take the country. The nobles, in turn, allowed the church to build monasteries and priories across what was a sparsely populated area. Needing a workforce to tend the sheep, grow food and look after the clerics, the church encouraged cottages to be built near ecclesiastical buildings and in time villages grew up.

Wool and cloth became synonymous with the area and most of the villages relied on this industry for their living. The men and boys tended and sheared the sheep. The women and girls graded and washed the wool before spinning it on their wheels, and from this yarn, cloth would be made.

There are many famous villages in the Cotswolds but from Oxford perhaps the most interesting and charming is the little village of Minster Lovell. You enter the village over a very narrow stone bridge. This and other such bridges were designed to allow the easy counting of sheep as the animals crossed on their way to market.

'Minster' is another word for monastery, but since there is no evidence of one here, perhaps the village's name indicates an administrative centre where the church's clerics were organised to work in other parishes. The land hereabouts was owned by the Lovell family, which gives us the name Minster Lovell today.

Once over the bridge, follow the river. To your left was an old mill, now demolished, but the miller's house still survives. Opposite is a pub, a nice example of half timbering. Up the lane that leads to the church and manor house are some charming stone cottages. In the spring and summer, the cottages are bedecked with roses, lavender grows in the little front gardens, hollyhocks spring up and buddleia shoots from the stone walls. A typical village of the Cotswolds will have stone cottages made from the local oolitic limestone, which is a beautiful mellow cream colour. The roofs are tiled in natural stone, rather than slate – which is mottled grey in colour and, as it ages, gathers moss and lichen. Here, though, you will see that many of the cottages have been thatched. In a farming community, as this was, once the harvest had been gathered, the straw was made up into large bundles and with this the villagers thatched their roofs. Not only did thatch keep out rain and snow but it also provided good insulation, helping to keep the houses warm in winter and cool in summer.

The windows, you will notice, are rather small; glass would have been too expensive to use on a farm worker's cottage, so wooden shutters were added to the inside of the openings. Often the bedroom had no ceiling. You just looked up into the thatch, which was an ideal place for mice to nest. When you went to bed, you could expect pieces of straw to land on you, and possibly the odd mouse that had lost its footing. So an old piece of cloth was often stretched above the bed, supported with poles, to protect the sleeper. From this came the four-poster bed, eventually with added curtains that surrounded it to give privacy and keep the draughts at bay. On thatched roofs today, fine chicken wire is used to keep out any small animals.

You'll notice there are no numbers to the houses here but many have names. This often reflects the original use of the house, so look out for the old bakery, the old post house, the forge and so on. Once the houses stop on your right, take the track that leads into the fields and, turning left, follow the footpath as it climbs gently to the church. Before reaching the church, go through the five-barred gate to your right and walk around the old fishpond, which will bring you to the fortified manor house. Built by the Lovells in the 1400s, this was known as one of the finest houses in Oxfordshire. It was U-shaped, around a yard, and faced the river, which would have been navigable in the time of the Lovells, with a little jetty where boats would have been moored. Today, the water laps over a small waterfall and the branches of trees drape into the shallow, sparkling water.

Surrounding the yard, the two wings of the house spread out from the main hall. On one side would have been domestic rooms, housing the kitchen, the bake house, brew house and stables. The facing wing would have been made up of a number of bedroom suites for visitors. At the end of this wing, a tower with its lookout still stands. The central part of the building consisted of a large dining hall and the solar (rooms used by the immediate family for sleeping or sitting) with a chapel on the first floor. Standing in the hall, you can see the bare stone walls rising majestically on all sides, but the timber roof has now gone. The height of the hall allowed a fire to be placed in its centre, the smoke rising into the rafters and escaping through the little windows in the gables. One such window can still be seen. Today, the walls have large holes, showing where different levels of floors and ceilings once existed, as different families renovated and modernised.

Walk through towards the church, which is dedicated to St Kenelm, who is known as the Cotswold Saint. This charming building, originating in the fifteenth century, is surrounded by a graveyard enclosed within a drystone wall. Following the path towards the road in front of you, turn left, go past the old rectory and then turn left again. On your right is the Old Post House, a perfectly proportioned house with a picturesque garden. From here, walk down the hill and you will return to the old bridge, where the Swan pub is well worth a visit.

Just a short drive from Minster Lovell is another beautiful village, Burford. Its name means 'defended settlement by the ford'. The village was predominantly agricultural but later became known for its markets and inns, where the coaches travelling through the Cotswolds would stop to change horses while passengers refreshed themselves with ale and food.

Its church of St John the Baptist was built, in almost cathedral-like proportions, at the end of the 1100s. It has a fine interior and some unusual tombstones, many of them in memory of the wool-merchant families who helped pay for the building's upkeep. When the railways were routed through the Cotswolds, they bypassed the

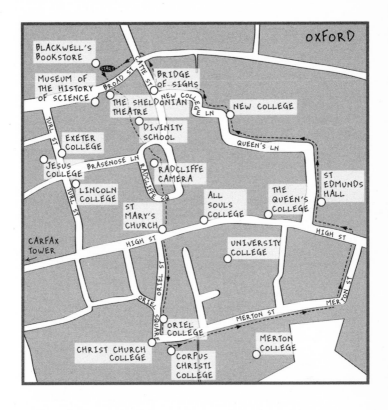

village. At the time, this was considered to be a disaster, but the village retained its ancient charm and honey-coloured buildings, and today it is a most popular place to visit, renowned for its teashops. If you fancy trying a Cotswold cream tea, try Huffkins in the High Street.

Bath – the waters of Sulis

KAREN PIERCE-GOULDING

'Oh, who can ever be tired of Bath?'
JANE AUSTEN, *Northanger Abbey*

The delights of the city of Bath are as bountiful as the bubbles effervescing from its hot-water spring. In fact, the whole reason for Bath's existence, right down to its very name, is inextricably bound to this natural fount.

Bath is the only place in the entire British Isles to have natural hot water gushing out of the ground – a million litres (220,000 gallons) each day at a constant temperature of 46.5 degrees Celsius (115.7°F). That's just the right temperature for a nice hot bath. It's been pouring forth abundantly for centuries.

Ever since the spring was discovered, the belief has persisted that it possesses magical medicinal properties, and if you bathe in the water or drink it, you will be cured of your ailments. This belief goes back to a Celtic tribe, the Dobunni, who lived in the area in the first century BC and worshipped Sulis, a water goddess associated with the spring.

But it was the Romans, those sophisticated southern European invaders, who popularised and exploited the spring. Once their invasion of Albion had succeeded and their main trading post, Londinium, had been set up in

AD 43, the Romans began to improve the infrastructure of their newly conquered territory by building roads. It was during the construction of the Fosse Way that they came across this miraculous hot-water spring at a place that became known as Bath.

Talented engineers, the Romans created a plumbing system of lead pipes to harness the spring water, and then built what they called the Great Bath, which was the size of a generous swimming pool, into which the water was released. As hot water from the spring continuously replenished the water level of the bath, excess water was led off for other uses – more baths, saunas and steam rooms.

The Romans also built a temple to worship the water goddess. Interestingly, they renamed her Sulis Minerva, adopting the Celtic deity by giving her a Roman surname. Their takeover was complete. The baths they called Aquae Sulis or the Waters of Sulis.

Today, a visit to the beautifully restored Roman Baths is an absolute must. They are the most vivid reminder we have of the Roman occupation of Great Britain.

Descending the stairs to what was street level in Roman times – roughly 6 metres (20 feet) below the level of Bath's streets today – it's not difficult to imagine you can hear the laughter and chatter of the baths' very first visitors as they splashed in the warm waters. The Romans loved to bathe, valuing the soothing and revitalising benefits of hydrotherapy. It was a favourite way to relax, not only health-giving, but also providing a place to meet friends, catch up on a bit of gossip or even finalise a business deal or two.

The lead used to line the Great Bath to make it watertight is still intact and the spring still gushes forth. As you walk around the bath's edges, you tread on paving stones worn by two thousand years of footsteps. Steam rising off the water swirls like the very mists of time.

Personal details in the museum rooms nearby really capture the imagination. A set of strigils (metal skin scrapers) and a pewter container for oil – the equivalent of our shower gel and loofah – a gold and garnet earring accidentally dropped by a wealthy bather, and piles of coins found on the floor of the baths, possibly thrown as offerings to Sulis, bring a presence to this ancient world.

When the Romans left these shores around AD 410, Aquae Sulis was all but abandoned. By the time the Saxons arrived in the late seventh century, the baths had fallen into disrepair. Not understanding the technology required to maintain the baths system, and faced with silting over of the site by a flooding River Avon, the

Saxons decided to abandon the baths and build on top of them. Luckily for us today, they didn't bother with foundations and so the Roman site was preserved.

Over time, layer upon layer of new buildings were constructed on top of the Roman site, and so although water from the spring was still used for its curative powers, nobody remembered the original baths, and they lay forgotten beneath the basements of the settlement now renamed Hat Bathu (Saxon for 'hot bath').

Centuries later, in 1878, the Roman baths were rediscovered by accident. When a gentleman living in a house in the centre of Bath complained of a leak in his cellar and a plumber was called in to investigate, a dripping, very old lead pipe was revealed to be the cause of the problem – an antique lead pipe to be precise. Recognising that there was something unusual about his discovery, the plumber called for a second opinion, and soon archaeologists arrived and began to dig and so excavated this incredible piece of Roman antiquity.

Arriving in Bath today, however, you are greeted by the eighteenth, rather than the first, century. The town was rebuilt during the 1700s, when Bath became the most popular holiday resort in England. The rebuilding of that time gave the city the elegance that is its enduring attraction today.

The chattering classes flocked here to take the waters and it became *de rigueur* among the upwardly mobile middle class to see and be seen at Bath. They were following in the footsteps of Queen Anne, who had first visited Bath at the beginning of the century. The queen was not a well woman – she had endured seventeen pregnancies of which just five went full term – and having heard favourable reports about the curative powers of the hot waters of Bath, she decided to sample them personally. Arriving in 1702 with her entire royal entourage, she soon became a Bath convert, returning on numerous occasions. (It could be that she was doing a detox without realising it. The queen was more than a little partial to brandy – the nickname given to her by the populus was Brandy Nan – and perhaps her feeling of wellbeing when visiting Bath was as much the result of substituting water for brandy as it was due to the properties of the water itself.)

Not all monarchs were as taken with Bath as Queen Anne. As you admire the grandeur of the Guildhall on the High Street, designed by Thomas Baldwin in 1777, it's easy to miss, almost hidden round the side in a lofty niche, a rather unflattering statue of Queen Victoria. It seems that town officials of Bath may well have hidden her quite deliberately, for although the attached Art Gallery was built in her honour, it is common knowledge that the queen hated Bath. Victoria had come here on a visit as an eleven year old, with her mother. She had been bored rigid and vowed never to return. She was true to her word, even snubbing crowds of Bathonians some decades later. The people had gathered at the railway station for a scheduled visit from her majesty but not only did the royal train not stop, it sped through the station with the window blinds of the royal carriage firmly shut.

Queen Anne, however, had given Bath the royal stamp of approval, and the rich and socially ambitious soon followed, all eager to try the waters for themselves. This enormous influx of wealthy visitors transformed Bath. Fashionable society wanted fashionable accommodation and, as a result, the city came to be rebuilt in the Palladian style that was much admired by the eighteenth-century in-crowd.

John Wood the Elder became the city's chief architect. He was inspired by the work of Italian Antonio Palladio and had always wanted to create a miniature Rome. In Bath, Wood's ambition could be realised. He settled in Bath in 1704, at the beginning of its building boom, and was given artistic carte blanche.

His *pièce de résistance* is known as the Circus, a circle of thirty-three houses, divided into thirds, a homage to all things Palladian. The facades, celebrating the main orders of classical architecture, are carved from the local honey-coloured limestone. This subtle golden stone was used throughout the city and became compulsory after Ralph Allen, the owner of the local stone quarry at Combe Down, became Bath's mayor in 1742.

It is this combination of uniform colour and style that gives Bath a divine harmony, making it appear almost edible and earning it the nickname of 'the golden city'. When John Wood died, his son John Wood the Younger continued his father's work, producing the Royal Crescent, a generous semicircle of Georgian houses with breathtaking views into Royal Victoria Park.

Typified by elegant curves and crescents of terraced houses adorned with graceful pediments, carved columns and pilasters, all lovingly symmetrical, Bath's architecture is now protected as a World Heritage site.

As palatial as these houses appeared, however, they were ostensibly holiday homes for the wealthy, rented for a few weeks during the season. Although impressive from the outside, inside they were quite plainly decorated with only the essential in furnishings, reflecting a time when the genteel were much preoccupied with appearances. Their concerns centred on what was right to wear, the right way to behave, how things, even one's house, looked from the outside. As well, of course, one didn't entertain at home, one went out.

The Pump Room, built by Thomas Baldwin in 1795, captures beautifully Bath's Georgian heyday. Designed so that visitors could take the waters in stylish splendour, chandeliers still drip from its graceful plaster ceiling, and one can still take the waters from the original fountain, administered by a pump attendant. Handel sonatas are performed daily by a resident chamber orchestra, effortlessly transporting the visitor back in time. All who dine here seem to sit up just that little bit straighter and behave just that little bit better in rising to this oh-so-civilised setting.

Presiding over the proceedings, if only in the form of a statue, is one of Bath's most famous characters, Richard 'Beau' Nash. The statue depicts him resplendent in long curly wig, waistcoat bulging over his ample tummy. Nash, perhaps more than any other individual, was responsible for the city's success.

He arrived in Bath bankrupt but with an astute entrepreneurial nose. Described by Oliver Goldsmith as 'an extraordinary charmer', Nash was sure that these wealthy visitors would soon tire of just drinking water unless they were amused. As Master of Ceremonies, Nash organised divertissements – dances, balls, musical evenings, firework displays, and perhaps most popular of all, gambling evenings at gaming tables. It all became an enormous success. People flocked to Bath as part of the social season, partly for their health but mostly to meet their friends, to dance, to gamble, to be entertained and, most importantly, to be seen. Nash understood that his clientele wanted to belong and to be respected, and he created for them a list of dos and don'ts, known as 'Mr Nash's Rules to be Observed'.

In addition to the spa, Bath also has a wealth of beautiful parks and gardens. On a soft summer's day, there is perhaps nowhere pleasanter than the beautifully manicured lawns of Parade Gardens with the waters of the River Avon gently gurgling and splashing through the arches of the Pulteney Bridge. The bridge is one of the city's most romantic landmarks. Built by Robert Adam in 1773, it encapsulates the eighteenth century's love affair with all things classical; it was the architect's own tribute to Palladio's rejected design for the Ponte de Rialto in Venice, and is Bath's very own Ponte Vecchio.

The gardens also provide a wonderful view of the gloriously golden Bath Abbey. A magnificent example of the final flowering of the Gothic style, this Perpendicular church was rebuilt by Bishop Oliver King in 1499 after he dreamed of angels descending from heaven requesting him to do so.

In winter, when the city looks like some gorgeous Regency Christmas card, you can do worse than tuck yourself into a corner of Sally Lunn's House in North Parade, the cosiest teashop in Bath. Find a seat as near to the crackling open fire as you can and indulge in a treat exclusive to Bath, a Sally Lunn bun. The teashop is the oldest house in Bath, dating back to 1482. Comfortably cramped, it is a safe haven from the biting breeze off the River Avon.

Sally Lunn was a young French refugee who settled in Bath in 1680. Finding work in the kitchens here, she concocted this bakery delicacy, which became the toast (excuse the pun) of the town! Below the teashop in the cellars is a museum with an original Georgian oven and baking utensils. The recipe is a closely guarded secret and, according to the affable staff, although many have tried to recreate the bun, none so far have been successful. Often eaten dripping with butter, this is a delicate balance of brioche and croissant.

Bath inevitably became something of a marriage market, a town where young ladies, as part of their 'coming out season', would attend the various balls, hoping to find their very own Mr Right, or even their very own Mr Darcy. Famously, Mr Darcy's creator, novelist Jane Austen, lived in Bath for several years, using her experiences of society in the town in two of her books, *Northanger Abbey* and *Persuasion*. In *Northanger Abbey*, Bath is described as 'a charming place ... with so many good shops', and the book's heroine, Catherine Morland, enthusiastically exclaims that 'I really believe I shall always be talking of Bath, when I am at home again – I do like it so very much.'

The Jane Austen Centre at 40 Gay Street celebrates the writer's life and works and is a must for devotees.

Returning to where we began this story of Bath, those who wish to take the natural spring waters today can do so at the Thermae Bath Spa, which stands across the street from its Roman ancestor. Open each day until late, there can be few better ways of whiling away an evening than to sink into the warmth of its rooftop, open-air infinity pool as the sun sets, silhouetting Bath Abbey and the surrounding Somerset hills. As you let the soothing water wash away the cares of the day, one of the city's mottoes springs to mind: 'Water is Best'.

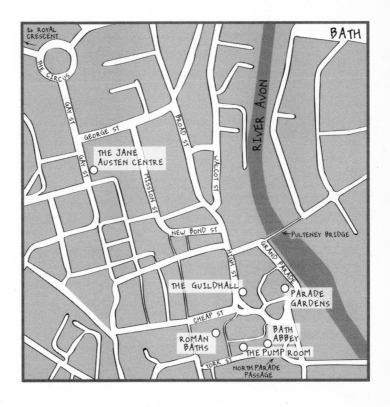

Rye and Battle – Smugglers and Invaders

CHRIS GREEN

A train journey through Kent, the 'garden of England', is a delight. The landscape is not rugged, there are no dramatic slopes, but the gentle undulations and splendid views over the downs make travelling a part of the day. This area is fertile, as evidenced by market gardens where small-scale growers cultivate soft fruit and apples – no vast fields of wheat or barley here. Charles Dickens described Kent as being full of 'apples, cherries, hops and fine women'!

Rye is signed as an 'antient' town. This goes back possibly to the reign of Edward the Confessor. He had no navy, as such, but needed ships to help him control the English Channel, and five ports were given favourable taxation benefits in return for these 'policing' duties. The original five ports found it onerous to carry out the tasks required and co-opted other towns as 'limbs'. Rye and the nearby town of Winchelsea, both antient towns, were given full membership of the Cinque (pronounced 'sink', *not* as in the French for five) Ports by the thirteenth century.

Today, it is difficult to believe that Rye was once a flourishing port. The river Rother has silted and changed course and the town is now some way from the sea. Winchelsea, which is situated on a hill and is visible from Rye, is even farther away from the sea.

Visitors to Rye naturally gravitate to the citadel, the high part of the town, from where the views over the marshes are stunning. On a clear day, it is even possible to see the bulk of Dungeness nuclear power station in the distance. This is Romney marsh, known for smugglers and for sheep – saltmarsh lamb from here is a delicacy. The sheep have adapted to living in damp pasture, unlike most, and at one time some of them were exported to Australia and New Zealand to form the nucleus of the flocks there.

Most of the houses on the citadel were originally built in the thirteenth century, although not much remains to be seen from before 1377. That was the year when the French raided the town and stole the church bells.

A return raid the following year retrieved them. Watchbell Street reminds you of the incident, as do the town walls, which were built following the raid. Two gates survive, the Landgate and the Ypres Tower. Rye has always had a tumultuous relationship with France. The town was once owned by the Abbey at Fécamp in northern France. Even after political and commercial changes, a part of Rye is still known as 'Rye Foreign' to remind the traveller of that relationship.

Several royal visitors have graced the town with their presence. In 1573, Elizabeth I stayed in the house with the crooked chimney near the church. She had such a good time that she gave Rye the right to call itself 'Rye Royal'. In 1726, George I was shipwrecked just off Rye, at Camber. The mayor of the town, James Lamb, put him up. This was very bad timing since Mrs Lamb was in labour at the time. However, the king, who was stuck in town for several days, agreed to be a godfather to the child, so some good came of the visit. Lamb House is still there, now owned by the National Trust.

As well as the royal connection, the house has a bizarre literary history. Henry James, the American novelist, bought the freehold in 1900, and wrote *The Ambassadors*, *Wings of a Dove* and *The Golden Bowl* here. He dictated his manuscripts to a typist, whom he apparently kept alert with the judicious feeding of chocolate. Local people remembered his loud tones rolling down the street from the garden pavilion, which was his preferred place of work. When he died, the house was let to A.C. Benson, who wrote the words of 'Land of Hope and Glory', and his brother, novelist E.F. Benson, who was a prolific writer, very well known in his day. He wrote the Mapp and Lucia novels, which are based in Rye and around Lamb House. E.F. Benson was mayor of Rye for a while, and also endowed the church with stained-glass windows in memory of his family. In one window he is depicted in mayoral robes, together with his black Labrador.

The church is well worth a visit. The climb to the top of the tower is challenging but, once there, the views are second to none. The church is often called the 'Cathedral of the Marshes' because of its size. Inside, a memorial to another of the Lamb family, Allen Grebell, can be seen. In 1742, in his capacity as deputy mayor, Grebell was standing in for his brother-in-law, Mayor James Lamb, wearing the mayoral robes. Local butcher John Breads mistook him for Lamb and killed him, while allegedly chanting 'butchers should kill lambs'. The mayor, the intended victim, presided over the resulting trial, Breads was found guilty and hanged. His body was left to rot in a cage for years on what was known as Gibbet Marsh, and what remains can be seen in Rye town museum!

Breads had his butcher's shop in Market Street, now a fine run of houses, many of which are hotels and eating places. This is one of the streets that was very popular with the local smuggling gangs. In the eighteenth century, many imported items were heavily taxed and it was therefore big business to smuggle these goods past the customs men. Having arrived at one building, the goods would be taken upstairs, through the roof spaces and out of a house several doors along under the noses of the customs men. Today, we have a romantic view of these smugglers. Rudyard Kipling has his version, as does Russell Thorndike in his novel *Doctor Syn*, the hero being a clergyman turned smuggler. In reality, they were desperate characters, responsible for huge loss of life and massive amounts of intimidation. The most infamous group was the Hawkhurst Gang, who met in Rye in the Mermaid Tavern. This is still a great meeting place, with its open fires, afternoon teas and decent local beers – not too many smugglers today, though.

It is easy to be sidetracked for days in Rye. However, Battle, which is in East Sussex, is our second destination, and the journey over the ridge of high ground from Rye immediately makes the history of the area clear. The

Battle of Hastings was probably fought on Senlac Ridge, although there is no sign of any battlefield, but more of that later. The B road into Battle is called Powdermill and this takes us back to an industrial past. Numbers of gunpowder mills operated locally until the nineteenth century, and plenty of evidence remains of poor industrial conditions and huge loss of life when the powder-making process went wrong.

From Roman times, this area was one of the most important places in England for the production of iron. As well as ironstone, wood, for the production of charcoal, and water were the necessary ingredients, and Sussex had these in abundance. The many ponds that can still be found hereabouts were not for ducks but for providing water for the iron-making process. Any large home in the area would have had firebacks made of the local iron, and ironmasters were allowed to have their grave markers made of iron. This is a real local idiosyncrasy and makes graveyards here unusual. Rudyard Kipling lived in a house that was originally built for one of these industrial masters. Many of the naval cannon to be used against the Spanish Armada were made here. However, water does not flow quickly in Sussex, and the industry eventually moved on to the north of England, where the fast-running rivers were more suitable for the iron-making process. It left its mark on the landscape, though, and until very recently, a commercial charcoal-burning operation was still working just outside Battle, used mostly for leisure items, such as barbecues.

The countryside also shows signs of another of our great industries – brewing. Beer is flavoured using hops. Hops grow well locally and until the middle of the twentieth century, hop gardens thrived in Sussex and Kent – 'gardens' because farms are liable to taxation. Hops grow on strings suspended between poles, and the poles are also produced locally in coppiced woodland. This simply means that the trees are trimmed down to encourage them to send up shoots, which grow long and straight and can be cut to make hop poles or hurdles for fencing. Hops are climbing herbaceous perennials and the female flower is used for beer flavouring. Picking these in September was always a labour-intensive affair and traditionally families came from south London to gather the hop harvest, employed by the same farmer every year, and often staying in the same 'hut'. Children were supposed to be in school, but nothing got in the way of the harvest! Even today, children from south London who are not in school for some nefarious reason will say that they are 'hopping off', probably having no idea of the history of the phrase that has been passed down through generations.

Hops have to be dried before they can be used in brewing, and this was the purpose of oast houses. These are the circular buildings with the odd, cone-shaped roof. The cone acts as a chimney. On the top is a vent, which can be turned to take advantage of the wind while the hops are being dried. These days, most of the oast houses have been converted to residential accommodation.

Far-reaching views are a feature of the road between Rye and Battle, which extends along the ridge between two river valleys. The rivers were once used for trade, but are no longer navigable. Sedlescombe, for example, one of the beautiful local villages just outside Battle, prospered through river trade throughout the middle ages. But the south coast of England was battered by storms during the fourteenth century. Water courses were re-routed and drainage channels dug, many of which have silted up over the years.

Before that, though, Senlac Ridge was at the centre of the crucial events of 1066. This was a very turbulent period of English history and, as ever, the accounts of it were written by the victors, so to find an objective point of view is not straightforward. We do know that William of Normandy fought a battle with Harold Godwinson on 14 October 1066, which has become known as the Battle of Hastings, although it is unlikely that Hastings was the location. Senlac Ridge is mentioned, which is near Battle, and it does seem obvious to name a town after a battle site. The really strange thing is that no physical evidence of conflict has been found. You would expect pieces of armour or the odd arrow head to have turned up. Nothing has been found elsewhere either.

The site that is generally acknowledged to be the battlefield is next to Battle Abbey, which was built by William. The story goes that he had vowed to found an abbey if God granted him victory. Sadly, there is no concrete evidence for this. It is more likely that the abbey was founded as a mark of Norman confidence in their control of a good invasion route. Whatever his reasons for building it were, William endowed the abbey with a collection of relics, his royal cloak and his portable altar. Much more practically, he granted the 'leuga' to the monks. This is all the land within a league, one and a half miles, of the abbey church.

The abbey is built right on the ridge – very clearly a good site for a battle, but not necessarily a great site for an abbey. Its situation would certainly have added to the building costs since massive amounts of terracing would have been needed, and water supplies would not have been straightforward. Apparently, building was started elsewhere and William demanded that the more difficult site be used because of the battle having been fought here.

Assuming this is the battlefield, it is easy to see the general topography. Harold's men were drawn up on the ridge, William's below. Both armies were more or less equal in size, bearded Englishmen, clean-shaven Normans, cavalry on the Norman side, axes on the English, both sides evenly matched in almost every way.

In the end, after many long hours, it was William's battle wisdom that won the day. As an illegitimate son, he had had to fight all his life and, amazingly, had never lost a battle. It was sheer discipline that won this one. His troops fell back, the English surged forward out of formation and William's men turned and enclosed them. Clever. There is no doubt about William's bravery. At one point when the Normans were not doing so well and rumours were rife that he had been killed, he rode along the battle lines, helmetless – foolish, maybe, but good for morale.

Harold was killed in the battle and the altar of the abbey church is meant to mark the place where he fell. This is not his grave, however, which may have proved a rallying point for those not kindly disposed towards

William. No one knows where Harold's body was taken, although there are plenty of legends. Today, the abbey church has gone, removed when Henry VIII dissolved the monastries. The stone that built it is visible locally, and it is noticeable just how many buildings in the High Street are made of the same stone as the abbey gatehouse – a good example of recycling. The abbey was given to Anthony Browne, a friend of Henry's. He turned one range of the monastery buildings into a country house, which is now occupied by a school.

The abbey and battlefield site are in the care of English Heritage, and a happy time may be spent, wandering over the ground, imagining the confict and reflecting on the fact that such a relatively small-scale battle changed the face of England forever.

Lacock and Avebury – timeless

John Blakey

Both Lacock and Avebury make great half-day destinations, and because they are just half an hour from each other, the visitor can combine them into a fascinating day out.

Surprisingly, many people don't know about the beautiful village and abbey of Lacock. And why Avebury, a prehistoric henge complex that dwarfs Stonehenge, isn't better known escapes me. If you have any interest in how we got to be who we are, how our ancestors used to live, or if you just love a good mystery, these are places you'll want to see.

On this day out, you can either visit Lacock first or Avebury, as you like, and then follow your own route once you get there – neither is so complicated that you'll get lost. We'll begin at Lacock.

About nine miles south of the M4 at Junction 17, turn off the A350 at the brown Lacock sign and follow the signs to the National Trust car park. There are two parts to this visit – Lacock Abbey and the village. I suggest you go to the abbey first, a two-minute walk, because the abbey is the reason the village is here. Follow the signs from the car park.

Surrounded by the Snaylesmeade meadows, the abbey is a wonderful construction, dating back to the 1200s. An abbey first, then a private home, it is now owned and run by the National Trust. The gardens are simple and frame the buildings beautifully. Wander past the small botanical garden and croquet lawn, pass the sphinx statue and find a spot to look back at the building. Note the sunken wall and ditch – known as a ha-ha – created to discourage sheep and other animals from coming on to the lawns.

Having been changed and added to over many centuries, there is nothing symmetrical about the building now. Its most striking features are the octagonal tower that connects the south and east fronts, and the heavy stone-tiled roof. And only time could create its beautifully mellowed golden limestone.

Follow the signs to find a seat in the cloisters. These seats were made for the nuns of the abbey. In medieval times, only monks, nuns, royalty and aristocracy were able to read and write, and these cloisters served as the nuns' 'office'. Before the days of gas or electric lighting, this is where they would work, the brightest spot in the abbey – with animal skins stretched across the glassless windows to keep winter winds at bay.

Look up. The bosses in the vaulted ceiling carry carvings of heraldic shields and grotesque creatures to keep evil spirits away. Nowadays, they attract fans of Harry Potter. Lacock Abbey doubled for parts of

Hogwarts School in the Harry Potter films, *The Philosopher's Stone*, *The Chamber of Secrets* and *The Half-Blood Prince*. It was here in the cloisters that Harry saw the image of his parents in the mirror of Erised. The rooms off the cloisters served as classrooms for Professors Snape and Quirrell. (You may also get a sense of déjà vu when walking the streets of the village – *Pride and Prejudice*, with Colin Firth as Mr Darcy, is one of the many films and television programmes that have been filmed here.)

Beautiful buildings can be admired, but it is the people associated with these old stones that fascinate. This abbey was established by a woman of great determination and substance, Ela the Countess of Salisbury. She founded an Augustinian nunnery here in 1232 in memory of her husband William Longespée. When he died, she buried his heart here ... the rest of him was buried in Salisbury Cathedral. William was the illegitimate son of Henry II and a witness to the signing of the Magna Carta in 1215, the document that King John was forced to sign, limiting his powers.

But Ela was not just a rich benefactor – the countess also became the very first abbess, rising at 2 a.m. with the other nuns for the first service of the day. Life was harsh; the only fireplace in the abbey complex was in the aptly named Warming Room, off the cloisters. In this room, you will see a huge black cauldron, nearly 500 years old and believed to have been used for cooking. The large stone tank near it was probably used for washing or to keep fish for Fridays. The Augustinians would not eat meat on Fridays, because that was the day on which Christ was crucified.

The abbey church was destroyed after Henry VIII broke with Catholic Rome and established the Church of England with the monarch as the head of the new religion. Subsequently, Henry dissolved the monasteries, seizing their lands, money and properties. In 1540, he sold Lacock Abbey for £782 to William Sharington, who transformed the vast open spaces of the abbey's rooms, putting in walls and ceilings, to create a wonderful family house. He also added the octagonal tower, where his valuables were protected in a strongroom behind a huge iron door. Sharington grew immensely rich, and as the under-treasurer for the Bristol mint, supplemented his income by clipping coins. Coins were made from real gold and silver in those days and clipping tiny pieces from them could net you a fortune over time. This is why coins have grooves or writing on the edges, so it will be obvious if they've been clipped. Sharington was eventually arrested for embezzlement, tried and convicted. His properties were confiscated and he was sentenced to death. However, by turning informant he escaped execution at the Tower of London. He was pardoned and allowed to buy back his estates.

As Sharington had no descendants, his brother, Henry, took over the abbey when William died. Henry's daughter, Olive, married Sir John Talbot, and it is the Talbots who, until very recently, lived here. The best known of this family is William Henry Fox Talbot, whose experiments in photography led to him making the world's earliest surviving photographic negative, which is of the oriel window in the south gallery of the abbey. There is a superb photographic museum by the main reception where you came in.

The abbey's last tenant, Petronella, left recently and the rooms still feel lived in, as though the family has just 'popped out', with spilled glasses of wine, unfinished jigsaws and letters half finished.

What of Lacock itself? Turn right out of the abbey and you will find a village without many of the outward trappings of this century, the last century, or the one before that, apart from cars, of course, and the occasional alarm box. You will be hard pressed to find television aerials, telephone poles or even road markings. In fact, not much has changed here since the 1700s. Matilda Fox Talbot, the last private owner of the abbey, gave the house, the estate and the village to the National Trust in 1944; this is why the village remains so unspoiled.

Lacock was created by the abbey as a home for the estate workers, and operated under abbey ownership. In the Middle Ages, prosperity was generated by the wool trade and Lacock grew into an important market town on the main route from Bristol to London – hence the disproportionate amount of pubs and inns! As you walk its streets today, imagine these same streets hundreds of years ago, when they would have been full of market traders and wool merchants. The town had butchers, bakers and its own brewery. The market cross is still here, in the school playground, reminding the traders that God was watching and to be fair in their dealings.

The abbey's numerous sheep provided meat and fleeces, which were washed in the nearby brook and in the River Avon. In old English, Lacock means 'small stream', a reference to Bide Brook, which runs through the town. The wool would then be woven on broadlooms. These occupied the first floors of many of the houses you're about to see.

The Red Lion pub is one of very few brick-fronted buildings in Lacock. The handsome brick facade is from the 1700s but the interior is of a much earlier date. Opposite the pub, the huge stone building is the Tythe Barn. Turn right into East Street and take an immediate right into the barn.

Most of the residents of Lacock would have been tenants of the abbey, so would have had to pay a tithe, or contribution, to the abbey, usually equal to about one tenth of their income. This was often paid in goods rather than in money, and the tithed corn, hides, wool, fruits or vegetables were stored here, in the Tythe Barn. At the far end of the barn is the town lock-up, used to incarcerate drunks.

Back out in East Street you'll see tiny stone-roofed cottages on either side, with tiny doors and tiny letterboxes, and also half-timbered Tudor buildings. Note the overhanging first floors of the latter. Houses of the time were taxed depending on how large the footprint of the building was. The trick was to build up and then out, to get more space without having to pay more tax.

Turn right at the end of the street, opposite the bakery, and on your right is King John's Hunting Lodge, the oldest building in the village, parts of which date from the 1200s. King John was said to indulge his passion for hunting in the surrounding forests and then to come here to rest and recuperate.

A little farther on is St Cyriac's Church – an unusual name, the origin of which is much debated. Locals favour the story of a three-year-old child of this name who was slaughtered in AD 303 for supporting the faith of his Christian martyred mother, Julitta. Do go in, if only to see William Sharington's amazing tomb in the Lady Chapel, adorned with his symbol, the scorpion.

Turn right out of the church gate into the gravel lane and at the end of this cul-de-sac you'll find the former workhouse, now a pottery and B & B. Lean times followed the decline of the wool industry and the workhouse became the last resort for many desperate locals.

Retrace your steps back into Church Street and walk past the bakery. Immediately on the right-hand side note the bulging walls and unusual doorways. The 'S' shaped metal brackets are all that are stopping the walls from collapse! You will see 'X's doing a similar job all over town.

The beautiful old inn on the right is called At The Sign Of The Angel. The angel in this case was the Archangel Michael, whose image could be found on one side of a coin much in use in those days. This lovely old timbered building still welcomes the thirsty, hungry and sleepy. Go through the old horse passage that led to the stables and out to the garden for a look at the orchard and brook. On a sunny day, a more idyllic spot for lunch is hard to find.

Bear left at the end of Church Street into West Street and on your right you will find the oldest inn in Lacock, The George, built in 1361. Low beamed and cosy, this pub's other claim to fame is the 'dog wheel'. At the side of a massive fireplace is a contraption like a hamster's exercise wheel, which is connected to, and turns, the cooking spit over the fire. Inside the wheel would have been a small dog, called a Turnspit, trained to walk slowly to ensure that the customers' dinners were cooked properly!

Crossing the road and turning left into High Street, you will pass shops on the road back to the car park.

* * *

And so to Avebury on the A4 and its prehistoric complex. This is the largest henge in Britain, containing the largest stone circle, a circle so big that a village has been built inside it, complete with thatched pub. A stone's throw away is Silbury Hill, the largest man-made mound in Europe, and West Kennet Long Barrow, where you can enter one of the longest burial mounds in Britain, dating back well before Stonehenge.

The path to the stone circle and village is from the National Trust car park. Within a couple of minutes you will see a huge ditch and bank. This is the henge. How did they build such an amazing structure so long ago? The sheer size of it can be difficult to comprehend. You could lose a fleet of double-decker buses in this ditch, and orginally it was even greater in dimension. The ditch is thought to have been 9 metres (30 feet) deep and the bank 6 metres (20 feet) high.

Neolithic man used the points of deer antlers as picks to break up the hard chalky ground, and then scooped out the earth using cows' shoulder blades. It must have taken an age. A generation? And why, about 2600 BC, when simple survival must have been high on the list of priorities, was so much time and energy devoted to such a project?

Walking around the circumference of the circle will take approximately twenty minutes. Get into the circle by turning right at the end of the path and right again, through the gate. Concrete markers show where stones used to be. Many of them are believed to have been broken up to build the village, or carted off to farmyards and used as blocks to help mount horses. The standing stones, just inside the huge ditch, are not 'worked' and shaped as they are at Stonehenge, and there are no trilithons (two upright stones with one balanced on top); nor were the stones buried to a considerable depth in the ground, as they are at Stonehenge. Instead, about 200 years after the ditch was built, these stones were simply hauled into an upright position. Crude, misshapen, often with their smallest side at the bottom, the stones were dug only a little way into the earth and so eventually fell over – or perhaps they were pushed. Did Christians, in late medieval times, vandalise this apparently pagan site? It does appear that some stones were intentionally buried. Fear of the unknown? Or perhaps they just got in the way of ploughing. It remains a mystery.

In the early twentieth century, archaeologist Alexander Keiller led a major excavation of the area and controversially re-erected ten of the stones. Beneath one, he discovered the remains of a man. Walk along the side of the ditch, with the stones on your left. The body was found under the sixth stone from the end. At first, Keiller thought the man was a tailor because he was found with a pair of scissors, a metal point, or needle, and some coins that helped to date the death to the 1320s. But in those times, barbers also performed surgery and so this stone is now known as the Barber Surgeon's Stone. Whether the man died as a result of the stone falling on him, or whether he was already dead and secretly buried, is unknown, but we do know that he had a healed cut to the head, possibly caused by a sword.

As for the purpose of the circle and its stones ... all over the world, stone has often been used to represent bone and death. Perhaps this was a place to honour the dead? Four thousand years ago, there were over a hundred burial mounds in the vicinity. And why circles? Circles have always been thought to have mystical qualities – they have no beginning and no end, so often represent eternity, perfection or God.

Now, cross the road into the next quadrant, using the gates. Turn right and head up the chalky steps on to the top of the bank. From here, you have a wonderful overview of the area from on high. You can see most of the village. Looking right, you will see some of West Kennet Avenue and the remains of a hundred or so pairs of stones leading to The Sanctuary, another former double stone circle. Looking back into Avebury Circle, the remains of two stone circles within the main circle are visible.

Avebury's outer circle once held around a hundred standing stones, and the two inner circles about thirty each. Inside these smaller circles were rectangular patterns of stones. The closer circle had a large sarsen obelisk at its centre, now indicated by a pyramidal concrete marker. At the centre of the far circle, on the other side of the village buildings, was The Cove.

Continue walking along the chalky path to the next set of gates and cross another road. Once through the gate into the next quadrant, turn left, keeping the tiny cottage buildings on your left. Two massive stones come into view. These stones have been known as The Cove since the early 1700s when antiquarian William Stukeley, the first president of the Society of Antiquaries, named them. Their exact purpose is unclear but the largest is about 100 tonnes, making it by some margin the heaviest standing stone in Britain. It may have been the first stone erected at Avebury and almost certainly pre-dates the digging of the henge.

Continue your walk across the road to the left of the pub, and down the slight hill. Pass the grocery store and gift shop, and you'll see the path to the car park on your left. Turn right instead and follow this path down past the National Trust shop. Nearby is Avebury Manor, where the lovely gardens alone are worth a visit. Near the iron gates into the manor is the entrance to the churchyard. Go through and bear left at the church of St James, parts of which are about a thousand years old. Continue along the path to the lych gate, which provided shelter for mourners and coffins, and turn left, then right, to take the path back to the car park. It is a short drive to Silbury and West Kennet Long Barrow.

Turn right on to the A4361. On your left you will soon glimpse Silbury Hill, an enormous man-made earth and chalk mound. It has been calculated that, using the materials available to them in around 2400 BC, it would have taken its prehistoric builders approximately 18 million man-hours to construct. Again, the question is why? Tunnels have been dug into the mound in a search for burials, treasures – answers. Absolutely nothing, except chalky earth, has been found. Some have suggested that the hill was used to monitor solar movement, using the shadow cast by the mound. The most popular legend is that a king called Sel is buried here, but he is yet to be found.

Continue to the first roundabout, which is just three-quarters of a mile from the Avebury car park, and take the first left on to the A4. The Silbury Hill car park is just half a mile up this road, on the left. There is more information about the hill here.

After leaving Silbury Hill car park, turn left on to the A4 again, and after 500 yards, park in the second layby on the right. Go through the gate on this side of the cottage and walk through the field (please stick to the path – this is a working farm). Go through the next gate and up the hill. You will see a long mound with some stones on the left. These stones are the entrance to West Kennet Long Barrow.

West Kennet Long Barrow is one of the oldest parts of the Avebury complex and was begun about 3700 BC. That is well before Stonehenge, a thousand years before the oldest of the Egyptian pyramids was built, more than two thousand years before Tutankhamun was buried, and more than three thousand years before the Mayans built their great cities in South America.

There are two main types of barrow – long and round. The round barrows generally contain a single burial. Long barrows – such as the West Kennet one, which is a 100-metre (328-foot) long structure – are for mass burials. Excavations have found evidence that the bodies may have decayed elsewhere before being placed in these chambers. Interestingly, the occupants of one chamber are nearly all adult males, and of another, young children and babies. Some bones have been taken away. So head into the excavated chambers now – if you dare!

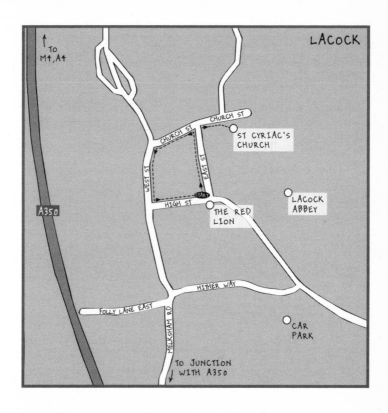

SISSINGHURST – FOR THE LOVE OF A GARDEN

GILLIAN CHADWICK

'When I first saw it ... I fell in love; love at first sight. I saw what might be made of it. It was Sleeping Beauty's Castle: but a castle running away into sordidness and squalor; a garden crying out for rescue.'

These were the words Vita Sackville-West used to describe how she felt the moment she set eyes on Sissinghurst in 1930. They say a great deal about her imagination and creative ability because the Sissinghurst of that time was a very different kettle of fish from the romantic Tudor 'castle' surrounded by glorious flower-filled gardens that we see today. With an abundance of hard work and determination, Vita and her husband Harold Nicolson transformed what was a set of derelict Tudor buildings, together with 2.5 hectares (6 acres) of wrecked land, into one of the most famous and loveliest gardens in England.

The first recorded settlement here at Sissinghurst was built during the Anglo-Saxon period, on a ridge overlooking the beautiful Kentish Weald. The tribe's leader, Seaxa, gave his name to the site – 'the people of the wooded hill of Seaxa', 'ing' meaning 'people of' and 'hurst' meaning 'wooded hill'. During the Middle Ages, a stone manor house stood here, protected by a moat, but it fell into ruin after the estate had passed into the hands of the rich and powerful Baker family in the fifteenth century. Parts of the red-brick Tudor mansion constructed by this family survive today, including the first buildings we see on approaching the gardens. These were the stables and servants' quarters, built in 1490 and converted by Vita and Harold into the long library.

The Baker family achieved their wealth during the turbulent Tudor period, when Sir John Baker managed to keep his head during Henry VIII's reign, supported Edward VI, and then survived the reign of Mary Tudor by relentlessly persecuting Protestants. Known locally as 'Bloody Baker' due to his penchant for seduction, rape and murder, nobody mourned his eventual demise.

Sir John's son, Richard, inherited and extended the property, erecting the four-storey prospect tower with two octagonal turrets that Vita imagined to be Sleeping Beauty's castle. Sir Richard welcomed Elizabeth I to Sissinghurst under this very tower, and then accompanied her to her quarters in the grand apartments of the courtyard, located where the gardens are today.

The power and wealth of the Bakers declined during the seventeenth century, particularly during the Civil War when Sir John's ancestors were not so adept at staying on the right side. Gradually the estate deteriorated until in the mid eighteenth century it became a prisoner-of-war camp for more than 3000 captured French soldiers and sailors. The conditions were appalling and in their desperate efforts to keep warm, they burned whatever they could get their hands on. So much was destroyed as a result that the main mansion was demolished in 1800. The only buildings left standing were the low entrance block, the tower and two cottages. It was these, together with 162 hectares (400 acres) of surrounding farmland, that Vita and Harold bought for £12,000 in 1930. Harold had initially advised against buying the property, thinking that Vita's heart was ruling her head and making her blind to the potential problems and expense, but it was Vita's money and the purchase went ahead. The place was uninhabitable at that time and it was two years before Vita and Harold were able to move in.

They started work immediately on restoring the buildings and clearing the gardens, but continued to live at Long Barn, their house situated near the ancestral home of the Sackville-West family, Knole. It was at Long Barn that Harold developed his skills as a garden designer, experimenting with the 'room' technique that we now see at Sissinghurst; and Vita's love of plants developed there, the embers of this passion having been sparked in the gardens of Knole, her childhood home.

In the library at Sissinghurst hangs a portrait of the eighteen-year-old Vita, painted by Philip de László at Knole in 1910. You can see that Vita was a beautiful young woman who could have had her pick of any of the heirs to great estates and dukedoms at that time, but instead she chose to marry Harold Nicolson, a diplomat and author. In the early years of their marriage she travelled with Harold to Persia and Turkey, where the two of them collected some of the ornaments later used in the gardens as focal points among the long avenues and vistas.

The Nicolsons' marriage could hardly be described as conventional. Vita had several passionate affairs with women, including Violet Trefusis, the daughter of Alice Keppel, who was Edward VII's mistress and the Duchess of Cornwall's grandmother, while Harold was equally active, having dozens of affairs with handsome young men whom he would dazzle with his charm and wit. But their marriage survived all these affairs and produced two fine sons. Vita and Harold were always the greatest of friends. (Violet Trefusis, incidentally, was characterised as the Russian princess Sasha by Virginia Woolf, another of Vita's lovers, in her novel *Orlando*, a book dedicated to Vita.)

Despite the delay in moving into the dilapidated buildings, Vita and Harold lost no time in creating the basic format of the gardens as we see them today. Harold was responsible for the layout and design of the ten gardens. Making use of three of the ancient walls that were still standing, and adding one new wall to enclose the 2.5 hectares (6 acres) of land, his classically inspired idea was to create a symmetrical pattern. He included long vistas along hedges of yew, box, rose and hornbeam, and pathways with small geometrical gardens opening off them, like the rooms of a house opening off corridors. Now and again, the eye is drawn to the focal point of a statue, a large pot, a flight of steps or a distant view of the countryside.

Once the format had been established, Vita's planting skills were able to flourish. In contrast to the formality of Harold's pattern, she filled the beds with an abundance of flowers, herbs, trees and shrubs in a riot of different colours. Vita described the plantings as 'painting with flowers', and every detail of height, texture and fragrance was attended to.

The garden was used as though it were a house, and to link the fragmented buildings of Sissinghurst. Vita and Harold's separate bedrooms and sitting room in the South Cottage were linked by the Yew Walk to their dining room and kitchen in the Priest's House; here also was a bedroom shared by their two sons. The long library at the entrance to the gardens was linked by the front courtyard path to Vita's study in the tower. The couple spent as much time outdoors as they did inside, so the garden areas really did serve as rooms. The front courtyard was the entrance hall, the White Garden, with its 'Erechtheum' – a covered colonnade named after a temple on the Acropolis – their outdoor dining room. The Cottage Garden was another sitting room for Harold and the Lime Walk was the equivalent of a stately home's long gallery. Vita and Harold never intended to create a garden for others to visit, although Vita was always happy to share her love of flowers with strangers who came to see it. The garden was primarily for the family, for their own use and enjoyment.

During Vita's and Harold's time at Sissinghurst the different gardens could be described as 'single season'. Each area was planned to put on a magnificent show for a short period, then when that moment of beauty was spent, another area would come into its own. For example, the Lime Walk, Nuttery and Orchard were spring gardens, the Rose and Herb Gardens reached their peak in the early summer, followed closely by the White Garden, while the Cottage Garden's fiery red, yellow and orange display continued throughout the summer and into autumn. This changed after Vita's death in 1962.

Vita realised that her family would be hit by heavy death duties when she died, so let her son Nigel know that she would understand if, in the event, he had to take certain measures to preserve Sissinghurst. Nigel decided to offer the estate to the treasury in part payment of duty, on the understanding that the property would be transferred to the National Trust. However, it was not a foregone conclusion that the National Trust would want it; some members of the gardens committee did not consider Sissinghurst to be one of the great gardens of England. Eventually, the fact that it was created by two great English authors, and also that it was considered 'romantic and intimate', saved the day and the National Trust took over the gardens in 1967, one year before Harold's death.

The single-season approach was abandoned in favour of having colour throughout the year in every part of the garden, in response to the expectations of paying visitors. This remarkable vision was brought about through the efforts of Sissinghurst's two head gardeners, Pam Schwerdt and Sibylle Kreutzberger, who worked at Sissinghurst for nearly thirty years, implementing the use of long-flowering varieties and tender perennials. Today, 200,000 visitors a year are delighted by the beautiful displays from spring until autumn.

Before we take a stroll around these fabulous gardens, let's just pop in to see where Vita loved to spend her indoor time, cosseted away from the world in her little study at the top of the tower. A spiral staircase leads up from the archway at the base of the building. Here she worked on her novels, including *Pepita*, based on the story of a famous Spanish flamenco dancer who married her grandfather, Lord Sackville-West, their marriage remaining secret until his death. She also wrote many gardening books and for sixteen years contributed weekly articles on gardening to the *Observer*. She loved to be alone, rarely allowing visitors into her inner sanctum, preferring the company of her dogs. The room has been left as it was when she died, with her books and personal belongings as she left them, including photographs of the Brontë sisters and Virginia Woolf.

Leaving the tower behind us, we enter the Tower Lawn, which has clipped yews and manicured grass; clematis and roses can be seen in great abundance trailing across the three enclosing walls. This area is not intended to be high-impact colour, but a formal space to contrast with the informal planting surrounding it. From the lawn, we can look to the right through an archway framed by a magnificent magnolia, liliiflora 'Nigra', its profusion of deep pink flowers harmonising with the mellow red brick of the wall. Here we see one of Harold's intended vistas – a straight line through the neighbouring Rose Garden and, at the end, a carefully placed statue, which defines the end of one path and the beginning of another through the Lime Walk.

Ahead is the Yew Walk, which we enter through a little gap. Walk to the left along the dark, tunnel-like avenue to another little gap. Turn left to emerge from the relative darkness into the brightness and beauty of the wonderful White Garden. Here dozens of different white-flowered plants are set against background foliage of silvery grey together with every possible shade of green, from the palest peppermints to the darkest emeralds. A multitude of heights and textures adds the finishing touch, making this garden a magical, unforgettable spectacle – a real feast for the eyes. It is not surprising perhaps that of all the gardens at Sissinghurst, this one is the most renowned and copied.

Vita first thought of a white-themed garden in 1939, but her original plan was to plant a part of the Tower Lawn in this way. Ten years later, she and Harold decided to implement her plan in the area between the Priest's House and the Yew Walk, which had formerly been mainly planted with roses. Harold designed the geometric pattern of box hedges and brick pathways and Vita made meticulous plans on how to fill the compartments to their best advantage. Nowadays, a different mixture of plants flower week by week throughout the seasons. The crescendo of this careful orchestration arrives when the rose that trails over the central arbour presents a mass of perfect white blooms in early July, making this the chosen period for any weddings in the Nicolson family. The happy couple greet their guests under the great canopy of flowers. Then, as this rose fades away, many of the other flowers in the garden reach their peak. It is easy to understand why the family chose to place their outdoor dining room in a corner of this garden, where they could sit and enjoy their meals in the warm, rose-scented air.

Going back through the gap in the Yew Walk hedge, we enter the orchard, the most natural part of the gardens. Sadly, many of the original apple and pear trees suffered the same fate as millions of other trees during the devastating storm that wreaked such destruction across the country in 1987, particularly in the south of England. But replacement trees are doing well, and during the spring the grass is filled with masses of daffodils and narcissi. The fruit trees blossom shortly afterwards, and later on, wild flowers show their heads among the grass, which is left to grow freely for a few months, to allow the bulb foliage to die back. This temporary meadow is a restful and charming place to wander through on your way down to the far north-east edge of the orchard, where you will find the gazebo nestling within the corner created by the two surviving arms of the medieval moat. This little summer house was built in 1969 and dedicated to Harold Nicolson, who had died the previous year. Its style is reminiscent of typical Kent oast houses, used for drying hops, that are seen scattered all around this area. Follow the eastern arm of the moat to its end for an opportunity to see spiky leafed, nettle-like hops growing in the Herb Garden, an area where Vita could indulge one of her greatest passions, cultivating herbs. She created her Herb Garden in 1938, enclosing four separate beds with yew hedges and planting each one with three varieties of herbs. Ten years later, over sixty different varieties of herb flourished, and now there are over one hundred.

This part of the garden is very high maintenance. Constant weed control is of particular importance, and some of the short-lived annuals, such as coriander and chervil, need propagating two or three times a year. The results are certainly worth all the hard work, though. The area can be full of bright colours, and intense aromas perfume the air. One of the precious pieces that Harold and Vita brought back from their time in Turkey sits in the centre of the herb garden − a shallow bowl supported by three lions.

We now start to make our way back through the gardens along the Moat Walk and Nuttery. Behind us stands a statue of Dionysus, the Greek god of wine, who seems to be surveying the scene from across the water. The Moat Walk is divided from the Nuttery by a bank of azaleas. Harold was not very impressed with Vita's insistence on planting azaleas. He felt that they were far too suburban for their romantic garden, but he gave in to Vita and the mature bushes provide spectacular autumn colour as well as vibrant oranges, yellows, apricots and scarlets in the spring.

Harold collected foxgloves from the woods at Sissinghurst to plant around the Kentish cob trees. He did not realise that he was also digging up bluebell bulbs, and so he accidentally planted these among the trees as well. Together with narcissi, polyanthus and primulas they created a gorgeous carpet of colour in springtime, but many of these plants were lost to soil sickness and fungal disease, so now a wide variety of wild flowers and woodland plants grows here in what is one of the least formal settings in the garden.

Harold and Vita were especially excited to discover a section of the medieval moat wall here, which predates the Tudor buildings and was probably part of the original manor house. A white wisteria tumbles over it like a glistening waterfall towards the end of June, making it a great favourite among family and visitors alike.

As we follow the Moat Walk, we are probably walking on what used to be a third arm of the moat in medieval times. We head towards the focal point of a flight of steps, decorated with four large Italian pots filled with white marguerites. These frame a garden bench that was designed by Edwin Lutyens, a famous architect and family friend. Lutyens was a source of inspiration to Harold in his design of the gardens.

Next is the Cottage Garden, probably the most intimate of the gardens and the one with the most personal memories. The garden lies in front of the first building that Vita and Harold lived in. The bedrooms were on the first floor and Harold's work rooms on the ground floor. The white rose they planted on the day they bought the estate in 1930 still flowers abundantly against the cottage wall. There is a cosy, secluded feel to this garden – a favourite with Vita and especially Harold, whose chair still stands by the cottage door.

In this 'sunset garden', the array of orange, red and yellow flowers may appear jumbled but the planting has been carefully planned so that the flower beds are bursting with colour for much of the year. From the wallflowers, tulips and irises of springtime, followed by the scarlet poppies, crimson salvias and burning red-hot pokers of summer through to the dahlias of autumn, the garden is full of rich, flame-like colour. The colours of the flowers are in perfect harmony with the stone and warm brick of the cottage and the paths, and the four yews provide a dark background to show off the sunset hues to their best advantage.

We now enter the Lime Walk, which is the first of the main areas of the garden to come into flower. A great profusion of tulips, daffodils, narcissi, fritillaries and bluebells burst into life, creating a magnificent carpet of colour within the strong architectural framework provided by the rows of lime trees. This is the only garden room that was not only designed by Harold, but in which he also did all of the plantings and much of the seasonal maintenance. A strong classical influence is evident in the statues at each end, and in the Tuscan pots spaced at regular intervals. These are often filled with bright orange 'Busy Lizzies', which provide a splash of colour during the summer months and a contrast to the green of the limes and hornbeam hedges.

As a final *pièce de résistance* we reach the sweetly scented Rose Garden. Originally, the Priest's House garden was used for Vita's ever-growing collection of roses. Then in 1937, the roses were planted here in what had been a kitchen garden for many years – the clay subsoil was rich and well cultivated, and perfect for rose growing. In the centre of the Rose Garden is the 'Rondel' consisting of yew hedges surrounding a grass circle. This effectively divides the rose garden into two, with Vita's rose-filled beds on either side.

Planting in the Rose Garden is different from other parts of the garden, where colours, form and texture are all equally important. Here there is little use of contrasting foliage but billowing masses of roses in soft and subtle colours. Many of Vita's favourite old-fashioned roses remain, their one drawback being that their flowering period is limited to one glorious month in midsummer.

Many plants have been added in the years since Vita died, so the garden is almost as enchanting before and after the roses are in full flower as when they bloom. Among the various herbaceous plants that fill in the spaces between roses, a few key types predominate. Lilies continue to flower for a few weeks of high summer after the roses are past their best. Tall, amethyst-coloured alliums stand like soldiers guarding the precious blooms, and copious lavenders harmonise perfectly with the pink and dusky purple roses. Irises, phlox and aquilegias are also used to fill in the borders and to extend the display throughout summer into autumn. A profusion of climbing plants cover the walls – Vita loved to see tumbling roses, honeysuckle, figs and vines – and today they include various clematis, valued for their late-blooming characteristics.

Here in the Rose Garden you feel the character of Vita's planting the most, in its soft abundance and rich, velvety sheens, and in the colours she loved – yellows and apricots, satin pinks, crimson purples and vibrant carmines. She would surely be content with how her glorious garden gift to the nation has been preserved.

WINCHESTER – A CULINARY TOUR

KIM DEWDNEY

No, not a tour of the restaurants, inns and eating houses of Winchester – although those with a gourmet fascination will find no shortage of places to keep them happy. It's just that so many of the stories of this city have a foody connection. So, for those people who are keeping an eye on their waistlines, here's how to enjoy Winchester while taking some gentle exercise; and for those who are not bothered, it's the perfect way to work up an appetite!

We start, as everyone visiting Winchester must, with Alfred the Great – or at least his statue. He's to be found on the Broadway by the Guildhall, where Winchester's current council meet to keep the city in order. It's an appropriate place because this is the man who brought education, religious instruction and defensive order to his people. Crowned king of Wessex in AD 871 at the age of twenty-one, he successfully held back the invading Vikings from his own kingdom, negotiating a border so that the Danes controlled the east and north of England, an area that became known as the Danelaw. The rest – West Mercia (today's Midlands) and Kent, in addition to Wessex – remained under Alfred's rule.

Alfred's royal palace remained in Winchester, from where he oversaw, and contributed to, the improvement of literacy by translating books on history, philosophy and religion from Latin into Anglo-Saxon, and established a legal code that was adhered to throughout his realm. He established an English navy, organised the construction of defensive towns (the footprints of which are evident today) and minted new coins, which referred to him as 'King of the English'.

So there is plenty to remember and admire Alfred for, but these achievements are not what instantly spring to most people's minds. No, that's the story of the cakes. Early in his battles with the Danes, after a reversal in the fighting, Alfred escaped alone into the woods of Wessex. Here he encountered a swineherd and his wife, who agreed to give him shelter and food, not realising to whom they were offering sanctuary. The couple worked hard each day, and while she was busy with other tasks, the wife asked Alfred to keep an eye on the cakes, cooking in the hearth. Alfred agreed but was distracted, his mind occupied by mightier problems. How was he to get his army together? How were the Danes to be defeated? And as he pondered such matters, the cakes burnt, to the intense anger of the woman, who came back to find her labour had been in vain. She shouted and scolded and the king submitted to her rage, knowing that he had been totally at fault. Once undertaken, no responsibility, no matter how small, should be ignored – that is the moral that has been passed down to schoolchildren for centuries.

From the Broadway, we now head to the riverside walk, accessible from Bridge Street (behind Alfred's statue). The bridge spans the River Itchen. The very first bridge on the site was built in the ninth century by a certain Swithun, about whom more later. The footpath along Weirs Walk has the beautiful clear Itchen water on one side and the medieval city wall on the other. The river is one of the finest chalk streams in the world and is a haven for wildlife, including otters. They come for the fish, and the brown trout, sea trout, salmon and grayling that inhabit its waters also attract fly fishermen and women from far afield. The river is depicted in a stained-glass window in the cathedral's fishermen's chapel, where Izaak Walton is buried. The window shows Walton sitting by the Itchen reading, along with the exhortation 'Study to be Quiet'.

His rod, keepnet and basket are at his side. Walton, buried here in 1683, was the author of *The Compleat Angler*, a celebration of the art of fishing published thirty years before his death. As well as direct instruction on how to fish, the book includes poetry, anecdotes and commentary, which has undoubtedly helped it to retain its popularity and remain in print for more than 350 years. Keep your eyes on the river here and see if you can spot any of Walton's prey. Walton preached patience and you may need to give it time!

At the end of Weirs Walk you'll enter College Street, where you'll immediately see the impressive buildings of Winchester College. But before we consider these, follow the signs to the right that take you towards English Heritage's Wolvesey Castle. One of the most important and largest medieval buildings in the whole of England, the castle was used as a palace by the wealthy bishops of Winchester. This coveted position was not only a top religious job but ensured that the holder was a major player in the political life of the day. Much of the land from here all the way to London, south of the Thames, was owned by the bishops and contributed to their immense wealth.

It was here, in July 1554, that Mary Tudor celebrated her marriage to Philip II of Spain, and he drank 'the tepid beer of the English, which does not offend them'. When it came to giving offence, Philip managed quite well. There was great distrust of his motives in marrying the half English-half Spanish queen, and many people worried that England would become little more than a Spanish dependency. What began with such promise was to end four years later with much bloodshed and no heir.

On attaining the throne, Mary had wanted two things – a husband and son to succeed her, and to restore her country to the true Catholic faith. She failed on both counts. Her marriage to Philip was not happy, and although she was deemed to have become pregnant twice, these are considered to have been 'phantom' pregnancies.

Her ambition to reclaim Catholicism for England meant doing away with the Church of England, which had been established by her father, Henry VIII, after his excommunication by the Pope. As Princess Mary, the only living child from Henry's first marriage, to Catherine of Aragon, she had seen at first hand how her father had dealt with good Catholics and supporters of her mother, such as Sir Thomas More and Bishop John Fisher, by ordering their executions. As queen, she was determined to address the heresy that England had exhibited under her father and her half brother, Edward VI, and she set about it with a vengeance.

Dominican friars came together in London to conduct the inquisition. Confessions from heretics were extracted using torture and the only punishment was death by burning. Many Protestant believers – including Archbishop Cranmer, who had assisted Henry in divorcing Catherine, Bishop Ridley, who had supported a rival to Mary, and Bishop Latimer, who had acted as Edward VI's chaplain – were burned at the stake in gruesome manner. A short – five-year – and sad reign on all fronts is what became of Mary, and you'll not find many people who feel too sorry for her. But perhaps this evening you can raise a glass in her memory, mixing tomato juice with vodka, seasoned with bitters, pepper and Worcester sauce, to toast an English queen with a Bloody Mary!

Retrace your steps now to College Walk and back to Winchester College. Winchester is the oldest public school in England. Boys have been educated in these college buildings since 1382. The school was founded by William Wykeham, Bishop of Winchester, and boys from the school are still known as Wykehamites. The original idea was to educate seventy poor scholars, who would progress from here to New College, Oxford, and eventually enter the ranks of the clergy, under-strength since the Black Death thirty years earlier.

Today's scholars are outnumbered by commoners, paying pupils. All pupils are boarders. The scholars live in the buildings you see here and the commoners occupy other houses around the city. The scholars are the only ones who still wear black gowns in school, making them immediately identifiable.

The houses are where the boys return for rest, recreation and food. The medieval college hall is where the scholars eat, and the benches and tables here remain nailed to the floor, doubtless to stop them being knocked over and to keep a semblance of order, given the clientele. A tour of the college takes visitors inside these buildings, including the site of the original brewery, which now houses the library. Both boys and masters drank beer because the water was too dirty. You'll also be introduced to the Winchester 'square meal'. Originally, the boys' food was served on wooden square platters – or trenchers – and they'll tell you these are the origin of the famous phrase.

Food raises its head again as we progress past the college to a small, privately owned house at No. 8. An oval plaque records the last days of Jane Austen's life. The writer, who described eighteenth-century middle-class life in such detail, paying great attention to correct behaviour, would have appreciated being so close to a school that has the motto 'Manners Maketh Man'. Mention of food in her novels is never innocent but laden with judgement and messages about the person supplying or eating it. In *Mansfield Park*, the clergyman, who should be full of self-restraint, reveals his true colours by providing turkey and legs of mutton for the local gentry on 'a great wide table which fills up the room so dreadfully'. Meanwhile, homesick Fanny is not settled by an offer of gooseberry tart, and a potential suitor is doomed to failure as he displays 'his Epicurism, his selfishness and his conceit'. In *Pride and Prejudice*, Mrs Bennett rushes to correct a misapprehension about the preparation of a meal, assuring everyone that she is 'very well able to keep a good cook, and that her daughters had nothing to do in the kitchen'. And Elizabeth finally realises what a great catch Mr Darcy will be when she encounters 'beautiful pyramids of grapes, nectarines and peaches' that have been grown in his greenhouses.

Jane Austen moved to this house in 1817, when she was forty-one years old. She was ill and her doctor was based in the city. She could now consult and receive treatment much quicker than when she was living at her country home in Chawton (a few miles outside Winchester and now open to the public). Her death has been attributed to many causes, including Addison's disease, cancer, tuberculosis and, in recent times, arsenic poisoning! 'Was Jane Austen murdered?' asked the *Guardian* when crime writer Lyndsey Ashford, having examined a letter by Austen, realised that all her symptoms were consistent with arsenic ingestion.

Murder is unlikely but accidental poisoning is certainly possible. In Jane Austen's time, arsenic was a popular treatment for rheumatism, an ailment that Jane talks about. Pills and preparations containing the poison were regularly prescribed, and could be bought from pharmacies. Lyndsey Ashford has proposed an exhumation to check on the state of Jane Austen's bones and confirm her suspicions, but this has been met with shock and horror by those who wish Jane Austen to remain resting in peace in the cathedral.

To reach the cathedral, move away from the metalled road and follow the footpath on the right into Cathedral Close. Walk right round to the west side, where there is a large stained-glass window and the visitors' entrance. To the left, on the ground, is a plan of the church that pre-dates this one, built in the 600s. It was in this church that Swithun acted as bishop in the ninth century. A holy and educated man, he was tutor to King Alfred and built the first bridge over the river. A miracle attributed to Swithun concerns an old woman taking eggs to sell in the marketplace in Winchester. On her way there she encountered the bridge builders, who frightened her and the eggs were dropped and broken. Swithun miraculously caused the eggs to be made whole so she could continue her journey. Inside the cathedral, a large screen behind the altar shows many prophets and saints, including St Swithun holding ... a bridge!

St Swithun's Day is celebrated, in Winchester at least, on 15 July. Swithun had asked to be buried outside the old cathedral in a modest tomb, and this wish was acceded to when he died in AD 862. A century later, in 971, however, when the church was enlarged and refurbished, the monks at Winchester decided to move his tomb inside in a grand procession. It is said that Swithun's disturbance at this denial of his wishes was the cause of a great rainstorm that started on the day his bones were moved, 15 July. The rain continued to fall for forty days and nights. Tradition has it that a wet St Swithun's Day will be followed by a long period of rain.

Doubtless, the reason for the monks wanting to move the bones of their beloved bishop had to do with their safety, but it also eventually made a lot of economic sense. Prayers were said at the new tomb, and miracles reported, so that eventually Swithun was made a saint and his shrine became England's second most important pilgrimage site after Canterbury. From the income these visitors contributed to the church, the monks and current bishop could pay for improvements, grand dinners and all manner of luxuries as well as day-to-day necessities.

As you leave the cathedral, stand with your back to the main entrance and you'll see a small archway that takes you through to the visitors' centre and the excellent refectory, where you can have lunch, afternoon tea or a refreshing cuppa. On the right, just through the archway, stands a statue of diver William Walker.

The whole of this area is marshy and, 900 years ago, the cathedral was built on a raft of beech logs. By the early twentieth century, the beech logs were no longer supporting the building, the east end was subsiding and the whole structure was in danger of collapse. The water table here is very high – the crypt of the cathedral is often flooded – and in order to dig out the rotting timber and lay foundations of concrete cement bags, William Walker donned the heavy diving equipment of the time and descended into the murky, dark water. The whole project took more than five years but secured the cathedral for generations to come. Walker is remembered today with two statues – the other one stands inside the cathedral. He received a rose bowl from George V, and was made a member of the Royal Victorian Order.

Now, to move from monastic austerity to the food of kings, follow the path out of the cathedral area to the High Street, turn left and walk up the hill to Winchester Castle, where the Great Hall dates from 1235, in the reign of Henry III. He was born in the castle in 1207 and returned here often. The hall was at the heart of the royal court, and more and more elaborate art and architecture were employed in its interior. Elegant pointed arches were made to hold up the roof, walls were plastered and decorated and the whole effect was one of brightness and colour. The king dined, discussed affairs of state and held court here, and administered justice.

On one wall hangs a huge board known as King Arthur's Round Table. Given that it was made in the thirteenth century, it's certainly not original – King Arthur's existence is a source of hot debate for modern historians. The table shows King Arthur at the top and includes the names of twenty-five knights, each with their own place. Sir Galahad and Sir Mordred sit next to Arthur, who underwent an unfortunate makeover at the time of Henry VIII when he was given Tudor robes and Henry's face! It's a table that would have done Henry proud. Weighing 1200 kilograms (265lb) and measuring 5.5 metres (18 feet) in diameter, it is a monster.

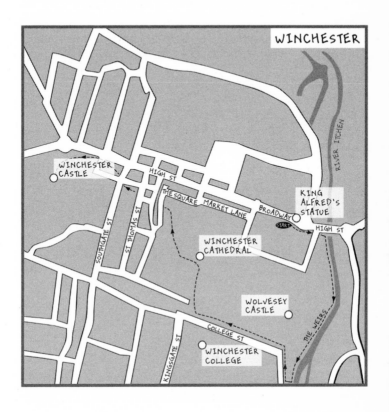

As you dine tonight, at a table of more modest proportions, think back to Swithun and Alfred, through Wykeham and the Tudors, to Jane Austen and William Walker, and others who have contributed so much to the history and greatness of this royal city.

HAMPTON COURT –
A ROYAL RESIDENCE

CHRIS GREEN

The only way to arrive at Hampton Court is by boat. You get the best views from the river, and can see clearly the difference in architecture that makes Hampton Court two palaces in one.

Of course, this is the way that the royals would have travelled here in the days when the monarchy needed to prove its strength, and it was a good idea to travel the country in company with a large entourage to show power and pageantry. Sixteenth-century palaces were generally massive and, with surrounding dwellings, could accommodate large numbers. Otherwise, if the king appeared with a thousand people in tow, you would quickly run short of space, resources and, not to put too fine a point on it, have issues with waste disposal!

Hampton Court was originally built for Cardinal Thomas Wolsey, who acquired the land in 1514 from the Knights of St John on a fifty-year lease for £50 per annum. Wolsey felt no need for a house that could be defended in time of war, and instead went for a prototype 'country house', using it as a brilliant piece of propaganda. Cardinals wear red, so his house was built of red brick. Chimneys were new and fashionable, so he ensured a forest of them, all different, were visible on the roof line. Once the news was out that he was building a house, gifts began to arrive from all over

Europe, including from the Doge in Venice. By the time it was finished, the place was sumptuous. You can still see Florentine sculptor Giovanni di Maiano's terracotta heads of Roman Emperors on the outside wall.

Henry VIII came to visit and liked what he saw. Eventually, when Henry required Wolsey to sort out his 'great matter' – his divorce from Catherine of Aragon – and Wolsey proved unequal to the task, the cardinal gave Hampton Court to the king in an attempt to placate him. It didn't work, but Wolsey avoided the executioner by dying on his way to London from York, in response to the king's summons. Henry made some changes and today his Great Hall is the centrepiece of the palace. It is a fabulous space, dominated by the original hammerbeam roof; and it has a fireplace in the middle, instead of using the newfangled chimneys. The roof has had a few problems over the years, mostly caused by conservation efforts, strangely. For example, the tannins in the oak were rotting the lead on the outside of the roof. Conservators decided to put in a 'buffer' layer of, basically, cardboard, but this was more acidic than the oak and reacted with the lead. As a result, the lead had to be completely replaced a few years ago, and at the same time an 'inert' layer was inserted between the two materials. As far as the visitor is concerned, the hammerbeams that support the roof allow a massive open space without the need for upright supports. It's even possible to see which beams provide the support because one of Henry's artists carved heads on the beams, looking down. Records show that they cost a shilling (5p) each.

Depicted in a thin line under the windows, known as the 'string course', are a succession of Tudor roses and portcullises (a symbol of Henry's mother, Elizabeth of York). This was one of the ways in which Henry emphasised to his visitors that he was in charge and legitimate. The windows, added by Queen Victoria in the nineteenth century, have coats of arms of all of Henry's wives and children.

Henry was a great patron of the arts. On the walls, a set of ten tapestries (of which six are on display) tell the story of Abraham. These come from Brussels and Henry paid £1500 for them. That may not sound much until you realise that a warship would have cost about the same amount! The tapestries are in brilliant condition because they spent a lot of time in the 'wardrobe', that is in storage, being put on display only when the king was in residence. Hampton Court has one of the most acclaimed textile conservation workshops in the world, where skilled crafts people are even able to wash tapestries the size of the 'Abrahams' without causing them damage.

The Great Hall was used for feasting, and later for theatrical performances and as a meeting place. Shakespeare's company, the King's Men, performed here for James I over the Christmas season, 1603–04, and James's wife, Anne of Denmark, used the hall to party. She apparently raided Elizabeth I's wardrobe and held theatrical extravaganzas at vast cost! Architect Inigo Jones was a friend of hers and, according to legend, built one of the first proscenium arches for one of her parties. James loved the entertainment, too, but on a more serious note, hosted the Hampton Court Conference in 1604 at which a new translation of the Bible into English was first formally discussed. The King James Bible was published in 1611 and remains one of the most highly regarded books in the English language.

Henry himself may not have spent too much time in the Great Hall. He had his own private dining room with a nearby staircase leading directly to the kitchens, so hot food would have been a distinct possibility. The kitchens were very modern for their time, as they needed to be in order to feed hundreds of people each day. They had huge amounts of storage space, bread ovens, charcoal grills and an open fire for cooking meat. Surrounding the palace is a deer park, an ideal source of food, and the river would have provided another. Deer still roam the park and fish, including salmon, have returned to the river now that the Thames has been cleaned up. The cooks were very good at flavouring foods, often because meat had gone off in the heat but could not be wasted. The kitchens today are how they would have looked in the reign of Henry's daughter, Elizabeth, and are sometimes used to put on demonstrations of Tudor cookery.

Kings and queens worshipped in the palace's chapel, where services are still held. Technically, it is a 'Royal Peculiar', just like Westminster Abbey. This means that the clergy are appointed by the monarch and have the right to wear red vestments. The chapel is on two levels, the top one for the royals, known as their 'closet', the bottom one for everyone else. The ceiling was added by Henry VIII. It was destined for one of the Oxford colleges and was being transported along the Thames when Henry spotted it and acquired it for himself.

The royals would have attended services in their closet, being part of the ceremonial but not in the thick of it. Henry actually married his sixth wife, Catherine Parr, in the closet here. He also used it as a haven when he had imprisoned his fifth wife, Catherine Howard, in the building and she escaped her gaolers to appeal for mercy. The corridor she ran along is still called the haunted gallery and she can apparently be heard in the dead of night. She's not the only ghost, obviously. The palace has plenty of them. Some are seen often and others survive only in legend or even nursery rhyme. Some obey the geography of an earlier building on site, which can be disconcerting because they go through walls, not doors!

By the seventeenth century, monarchs had less power and not so much need for so many huge dwellings in which to demonstrate it. However, Hampton Court was perfect for William of Orange, who came to the throne together with his wife Mary in 1689. William had asthma and was not a strong walker. The flat land of Hampton Court reminded him of Holland, and the air quality was good. He commissioned Christopher Wren to knock down the old-fashioned building and create a new one. He also asked Wren to work on Kensington Palace for him, choosing that area for the same reason of healthy air quality.

Normally in a royal palace, a suite of rooms is set aside for the monarch and a less sumptuous suite for the consort. William and Mary were joint and equal rulers and so two equal suites of rooms had to be built. Unfortunately for Mary – and luckily for us – she died before the project was completed, which is why half the palace dates back to the sixteenth century and half dates from two hundred years later. The two very different styles of architecture are in unhappy juxtaposition in some places, and the sheer size of the palace is difficult to appreciate unless you happen to be in a hot air balloon!

Christopher Wren found materials difficult to obtain, so he built in red brick with stone on the corners and around the windows. This is striking and relatively cheap. Many public buildings in Britain are built in this style today for those reasons. Sometimes, it is even nicknamed the 'Wrenaissance' style! Apparently, William often thought of himself as Herakles, the strong Greek god, and so Herakles appears all over the building. Perhaps the representations are William personified?

At this time, the king would have had a set of semi-public rooms, known as an 'enfilade'. Depending on a visitor's importance, he would travel farther down the row of rooms. The most private of them was the bedchamber, or 'cabinet', and the king would have been put to bed here by his closest advisers. These days, the prime minister's closest advisers are members of the cabinet, which is a lovely example of how language evolves.

At Hampton Court, the enfilade was on the first floor, or 'piano nobile'. The king would have to climb stairs to it, not easy for William, so his architect dropped the ceilings of the ground floor, making it less far to go. If you climb the main staircase, the risers are almost too shallow until you get into a rhythm. While climbing, you are surrounded by a wall painting designed to show how wonderful England was with William on the throne. This is the theme of the whole enfilade. The guard chamber is a riot of weaponry, artistically arranged to show power and strength, and with a splendid portrait of William, showing him looking physically very strong and surrounded by adoring girls and overflowing horns of plenty – a portrayal that was possibly a little economical with the truth!

The rooms today are much as they would have been in William's day. They were restored close to the original after a big fire in the 1980s. In fact, the fire was a major stimulus for craft skills that had almost died out. There was a fire at Windsor Castle at almost the same time and both of these restorations required large numbers of skilled craftsmen and women. At Hampton Court, a conscious decision was made to reclaim as much as possible from the fire and re-use it. The mirrors and chandeliers are the originals and the drapes were woven on seventeenth-century looms. The wardrobes (store rooms) at Windsor Castle were raided for tapestries and candle sconces, which would have adorned the building originally. Luckily, no tapestries were hanging in the rooms at Hampton Court at the time of the fire, but the knowledge that it would have been impossible to remove them caused some disquiet. Now all tapestries are hung using Velcro for ease of speedy removal. This is also the case in most other 'heritage' properties where insurance is a problem.

Walking through the enfilade, there is a brilliant view of the privy garden, which has been restored to its 1702 design and so is as William would have known it before his successor, Mary's sister Anne, had it dug up because, apparently, she hated the smell of box wood. In the 1990s it was decided to re-make the garden in its original form. Plans for it existed and garden archaeologists were called in to look at some of the surviving root structures to see how the planting had been figured.

Lancelot 'Capability' Brown was appointed master gardener at Hampton Court by George III in 1764, and held that position until his death nearly twenty years later. He planted the Great Vine in 1768 and it is still flourishing. The grapes it produces are for sale each year. Originating from just one plant, it has its own greenhouse and the surrounding soil is not cultivated so that its nutrition is not compromised. The gardens in general are a riot of colour from early spring right through to the autumn, especially when they are competing with the 'show' gardens put together for the Hampton Court flower show every summer.

Gradually, Hampton Court came to be seen as useful living space for retired royal servants, and indeed retired civil servants and ambassadors who may have fallen on hard times. They were allowed to stay at Hampton Court by the 'Grace and Favour' of the monarch. So many lived there in the nineteenth century that Queen Victoria nicknamed the building the Royal Squat! These days, when such an arrangment is no longer financially viable, just a few people have apartments in the palace.

Queen Victoria opened Hampton Court to the public and carried out her own refurbishment, including the windows in the Great Hall. Her ideas coincided with the opening of the railway, so access became easier and cheaper for all. Travelling by rail is nowhere near as much fun as arriving by river, though. If you were being transported by a crack team rowing with the tide, you could almost have beaten the train. Those were the days!

STRATFORD-UPON-AVON – A TALE OF SHAKESPEARE

NICK DAY

Welcome to my world – well, for the time being anyway. As I write this, I'm sitting in my little cottage on Waterside, and the iconic three letters that still strike wonder and longing in my heart shine down on me from the façade of the Royal Shakespeare Company – RSC. I'm lucky to be working with the Royal Shakespeare Company in a very special year. When I was here last it was another special year, and at the conclusion of that immensely successful 2006 Complete Works season, the theatre spilled its sated audience on to the street for the last time before undergoing a bold and comprehensive transformation.

Now, while celebrating fifty years since the foundation of the most famous theatre company in the world, the RSC has triumphantly welcomed audiences back into what I am sure will be acknowledged as a theatre for all time. Let's imagine that you have come to visit me here and have asked me to show you around.

If you have travelled by road, you will almost certainly have come from the M40 and been denied the pleasure of crossing the very bridge that would have marked the end of Shakespeare's long journeys home from his London base. The 'great and sumptuous bridge across the Avon' – built at the end of the fifteenth century, with fourteen arches – was funded by local man made good, Sir Hugh Clopton. It's fearfully narrow and pedestrians can also use its brick-built neighbour, which once carried an early nineteenth-century horse tram to Moreton-in-Marsh. But my visitors' first sight of Stratford is most likely to be the frankly unexciting multi-storey car park on the town side of the river.

In a town littered with representations of Shakespeare, the first thing to tick off on your personal bardathon, visible as you come round the bend, is the Gower Memorial, named after its designer, Lord Ronald Sutherland-Gower, who donated it to the town – after working on it for no less than twelve years. It was unveiled by the great actor Henry Irving in 1888. The memorial stands in Bancroft Gardens (named after nobody – it was formerly 'Bank Croft') and is flanked by the figures of Hamlet, Lady Macbeth, Falstaff and Prince Hal. Shakespeare's plays were not customarily performed in the town of his birth. Bizarrely, David Garrick's 1769 Shakespeare Festival, the first major exercise of bardolatry for Stratford, included a celebratory horse race, but no performance of a play. Charles Edward Flower, whose successful brewery stood alongside the Stratford-upon-Avon canal, must take credit for a Shakespearean enterprise, now of industrial proportions, that is worth £58 million a year to the regional economy.

Charles Edward Flower's father, Edward Fordham Flower, founded Flower's brewery here in 1831, a wise decision when it came to distribution. Stratford lies at the very centre of England, close to the major conurbations of the Midlands with excellent transport links to a large swathe of towns and villages. The town's position at the end of the canal system connected it to a wide market. The river Avon reaches from the west coast right into the heart of the country and, as the town's name implies, there has long been a ford across it here. In the nineteenth century, the Avon was made navigable from Bristol to Stratford, and the canal network joined to the Stratford Basin right under Clopton Bridge.

Charles Edward Flower joined the staff at the family brewery at the age of fifteen, as the family's brewing fortune started to look secure. *Punch* magazine was to judge their beer 'about the best produced in England'. Charles Edward clearly had beer running through his veins, and generosity spilling from his soul, for he purchased and donated the land so that a splendid and elaborate theatre could be built. It opened in 1879 with a production of *Much Ado About Nothing*, in which Helen Faucit gave her celebrated Beatrice at the age of sixty-seven!

The Shakespeare Memorial Theatre was designed by William Unsworth in a style that would earn comparison with a German fairy-tale castle. Sadly, after less than fifty years, a catastrophic fire rendered it inoperable, but much of the exterior remains today and we can visually dissect it from the twentieth-century Shakespeare Festival Theatre that was grafted on to it. A fascinating potpourri of detail remains to delight us – some Gothic, some Tudor – on a basically red-brick structure. The valuable Shakespeare Memorial Library was housed in what is now the Swan Theatre bar. We can still ascend the stairs from the original foyer, leading to the grand saloon, where the lancet windows lead us through the seven ages of man. The last age of all – sans teeth, sans eyes, sans everything – is, naturally, the window nearest to heaven.

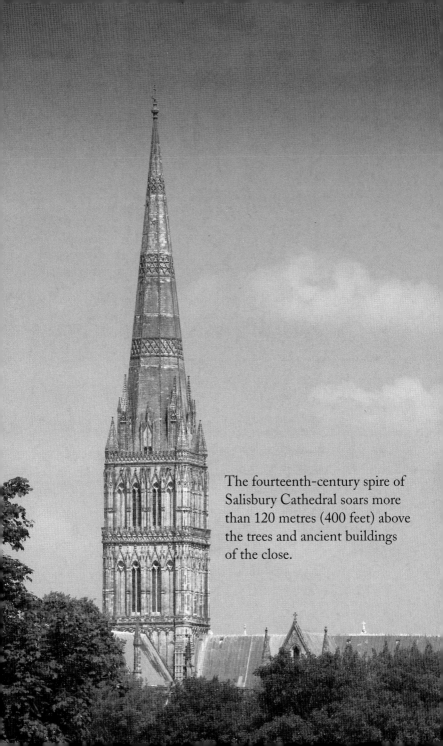

The fourteenth-century spire of
Salisbury Cathedral soars more
than 120 metres (400 feet) above
the trees and ancient buildings
of the close.

The charming scene of the River Stour and Lott's cottage depicted in John Constable's much-loved 1821 painting *The Hay Wain* (*above*) is little changed today (*below*).

The code-breaking successes at Bletchley Park – particularly the breaking of the Enigma code – played a decisive part in shortening the Second World War. Central was the work of cryptanalyst Alan Turing, who is immortalised at Bletchley in Stephen Kettle's intriguing slate sculpture.

Silbury Hill in Wiltshire, a man-made chalk and clay mound, was constructed around 4,500 years ago and is the tallest Neolithic monument in Europe. Archaeologists are unsure of its exact purpose.

The origins of Stonehenge are thought to go back to 3000 BC, predating the setting of the stones in the circle, which took place some hundreds of years later.

The creation of Vita Sackville-West and Harold Nicolson, the gardens of Sissinghurst are among the loveliest in England.

The Garrick Inn in Stratford-upon-Avon is named after eighteenth-century actor-manager David Garrick, whose 1769 Shakespearian festival in Stratford popularised the Bard and helped to create today's Shakespeare industry.

The plaque outside the 'Six Poor Travellers' house in Rochester commemorates the charity of Richard Watts in providing a meal, a bed for the night and four pence for destitute travellers.

RICHARD WATTS ESQ[R]

BY HIS WILL DATED 22nd AUGUST 1579
FOUNDED THIS CHARITY.
FOR SIX POOR TRAVELLERS
WHO NOT BEING ROGUES OR PROCTORS
MAY RECEIVE GRATIS FOR ONE NIGHT
LODGING ENTERTAINMENT
AND FOUR PENCE EACH
IN TESTIMONY OF HIS MUNIFICENCE
IN HONOUR OF HIS MEMORY
AND INDUCEMENT TO HIS EXAMPLE
THE CHARITABLE TRUSTEES OF THIS CITY
AND BOROUGH HAVE CAUSED
THIS STONE TO BE RENEWED
AND INSCRIBED
A.D. 1865:

The Roman baths in Bath were rediscovered in the nineteenth century after being built over and forgotten for many hundreds of years.

This eighteenth-century street plan of Bath shows the Circus, location of the famous Palladian-styled houses designed by the city's chief architect, John Wood the Elder. It also shows the Royal Crescent, an iconic semi-circle of Georgian architecture designed by his son, John Wood the Younger.

Weirs Walk is to be found on the pretty River Itchen in Winchester.

On the outside of the building, above the old library, is a Juliet balcony with terracotta panels depicting scenes from *Hamlet*, *King John* and *As You Like It* – a tragedy, history and comedy. It might be fun for you to work out which is which. At the flat end of the apsidal section of the building with the steeply pitched roof, there was a standard proscenium 'picture frame' stage that an actor could traverse in just eight paces. The fine roof we see today replaced the one that was destroyed in the fire. The building had an extravagant turreted tower, which, ingeniously, held a large tank of water designed to help extinguish any outbreak of fire. As it turned out, in the fire that was to consume the theatre in 1926, the tower acted as a highly efficient chimney and was burned down before the water could be deployed. So the theatre that Oscar Wilde described as 'a beautiful building, one of the loveliest erected in England in many years' was suddenly an empty burned-out shell.

It is tempting to examine the brave new Royal Shakespeare Theatre with its aspiringly iconic observation tower, but we should spend a little time talking about Elizabeth Scott and the art deco detail in the radical building she designed to inherit the mantle of the annual Shakespeare Festival in the 1930s. Elizabeth, at the age of twenty-nine, won the competition to design a valuable and lasting celebration of the greatest ever English writer. The exterior of her building is both admired and abhorred, but her interior design is up there with the finest of the art deco period. Elizabeth was second cousin to the great architect Sir Giles Gilbert Scott, whose principal oeuvre was the Anglican cathedral in Liverpool, begun in 1903 and finally completed in 1978. Elizabeth's building was to have an easier ride, and it became very much an expression of its time. Lovers of art deco will delight in the green Swedish marble staircase, the steel and brass box office, the foyer clock, the exquisite marquetry on the doors to the Ruinart champagne bar, together with a host of interesting detail, such as the bronze studs around the exterior doors and the imaginative treatment of the brick river elevation.

Lovers of theatre, however, were never delighted by the performance space. It was to become one of the least-loved stages in one of the best-loved theatres in the world. From the time the theatre opened in 1932, a succession of frustrated artistic directors wrestled with the space in attempts to address the problems it presented to both actor ('the forestage is an unbridgeable gulf') and audience ('sitting at the back of the circle was like being a spectator at someone else's party'). The director of the first Shakespeare Festival to be staged in the building described it as 'the theatre, of all theatres in England, in which it is hardest to make an audience laugh or cry'.

During the following years attempts were made to right the problem. Peter Hall, who founded the Royal Shakespeare Company in 1961, envisaged creating an amphitheatre-style stage inside the cavernous auditorium, but a good and proper – and feasible – solution to the theatre's intractable difficulties could not be found. In 1998, artistic director Adrian Noble announced plans to demolish the whole building and start over. So radical was his plan, conceived at a time when the RSC was suffering a £2.8 million deficit, that it was destined to fail. The hiatus of a complete rebuild could have been fatal to a company that employed some 700 people and had become a vital part of the local economy.

Trevor Nunn, during his tenure at the RSC, had been determined to create a smaller, thrust-stage theatre within the shell of the old nineteenth-century auditorium. Such a theatre would be suitable for the performance of the consciously theatrical plays of Shakespeare and his contemporaries. In 1983, a wealthy American visitor, Frederick Koch, who had already sponsored the Picture Gallery in the old theatre saloon, spotted a model of the proposed new theatre, imaginative and galleried, in an exhibition there. Three years later, he stood proudly alongside the Queen when she opened the theatre that owed everything to him. The intimate, wooden Swan Theatre was to become dear to actors and audiences alike who met together in the uncluttered playing space, and its thrust-stage configuration became the model for the future Royal Shakespeare Theatre.

The Royal Shakespeare Theatre building of today is the result of one man's vision and determination. It was the current artistic director, Michael Boyd, who managed to convince everybody who mattered that it would be possible to create a theatre within Elizabeth Scott's building – a theatre in which plays, that had originally been written for a stage where there was no barrier between actor and audience, could be most effectively performed.

From 2007–11, the £112 million Transformation project made a long-nurtured dream real – a modern theatre suited to the performance of Shakespeare's plays. The temporary Courtyard Theatre, built in a huge iron shed in a former car park a little way down the road, maintained the continuity of theatrical enterprise in the town. This stop-gap building followed the same thrust-stage configuration and was to be an immensely useful transitional model for the new theatre space that was still subject to modification on the drawing board.

So here it is – a new building for Stratford. Let's go in via the welcoming glass frontage and admire the now cherished art deco interior. The new observation tower has a somewhat uncompromising presence, but from its viewing gallery we can see no less than four counties – and my back garden. I would recommend getting an idea of the layout and size of Stratford before you do any more exploring.

Having got the lie of the land, it's probably a good idea to head off to Shakespeare's birthplace in Henley Street. If you go towards the medieval Clopton Bridge, then turn left up Bridge Street, you'll be walking into the heart of Shakespeare's Stratford. Taking a right fork at Barclays Bank (once the Market House) will take you up past practitioners of that oddest and most idle of professions, the human statue, to the home of the bard's parents. You can buy an all-inclusive five-property ticket that will gain you entrance to William's birthplace, where his first cry was heard in April 1564, and enable you to join the slow procession through the imaginatively re-created interior. This includes the glover's workshop where Will's father cured goat leather in buckets of dog poo.

In the untreated wood and buff-colored infill of the building you can see what the traditional half-timbered buildings of England really looked like, before the Victorians painted the timbers black and the plaster white. In fact, Stratford has a plethora of handsome nineteenth-century 'Tudorbethan' buildings to admire during this walk. The Shakespeares' house in Henley Street was built in the late 1400s or early 1500s and looks very much as it did when its appearance was first recorded for posterity in 1769, about 150 years after Shakespeare's death. The oak beams come from the nearby Forest of Arden. Some idea of the wealth and status of a house-owner of those times could be gained from the amount of timber incorporated that was not structurally necessary. The sides of this house, which, since it was originally part of a continuous terrace, were not visible, are sparely 'balloon-framed'. The street elevation, however, has more timber on show, and the ground floor is actually 'close-studded'. The non-structural 'studs' express the status of Shakespeare's father as alderman and subsequently high bailiff (effectively mayor) of Stratford.

John Shakespeare had a humble beginning as a farmer's son but after joining the 'mystery, craft or occupation of the Glovers, Whittawers and Collarmakers' he rose to become, for a time, the most important man in the town. He married well, too. Mary Arden had inherited considerable wealth and her inheritance included a good quantity of painted wall hangings, oxen, bullocks, cows, calves, sheep, bees and poultry. One of John Shakespeare's civic duties was to arrange licensing, accommodation and fees for visiting theatrical performers. We can imagine that he would have been especially proud to take his young son to see the Queen's Men, who had managed to negotiate a fee nine times more than the Earl of Worcester's Men in the same year.

Next door to the house in Henley Street is the Shakespeare Centre, opened in 1964 to commemorate the bard's quatercentenary. This is the headquarters of the Birthplace Trust and an educational centre, which holds tens of thousands of publications in its library together with a 1623 First Folio and thirty-one priceless contemporary Shakespeare records.

Walking back down Henley Street, you'll see on the left the public library, saved from demolition in 1901 by Andrew Carnegie. Born in Scotland in 1835, he founded the Carnegie Steel Company in Pittsburgh, Pennsylvania, in the late nineteenth century, and funded many schools, universities and libraries in the US and the UK from his vast wealth. He is often regarded as the second richest man in history.

Turning right at Barclays Bank will take you along High Street, Chapel Street and then Church Street. On the way you will pass some attractive half-timbered buildings in High Street and see ahead of you the eighteenth-century Cotswold stone Town Hall. Here you will find the statue of Shakespeare donated by the great Shakespearian actor-manager David Garrick in 1769 when he staged the three-day festival that really founded the modern Shakespeare tourism industry. In tribute to this celebrated 'bardolator', the Greyhound Inn was renamed The Garrick.

For a small and impoverished town, Stratford has always been well supplied with pubs. At the time when Shakespeare was displaying his considerable wealth and success by purchasing the grandest townhouse on the market, the Stratford elders castigated alehouse keepers for selling alcohol of unreasonable strength, leading to the 'increase of quarrelling and other misdemeanors in their houses and the farther and greater impoverishment of many poor men haunting the said houses when their wives and children are in extremity of begging.' One third of the population was on the poor lists.

It was at this very inn, the Greyhound, in the year Shakespeare was born, that an outbreak of plague claimed its first victim, the burial entry in the parish register noting '*hic incepit pestis*'. That outbreak went on to take one seventh of the local population. Baby William survived but various other plagues were to carry off three of his siblings in their infancy and, in London, his actor brother Edmund at the age of twenty-seven.

The steeply gabled and jettied Garrick Inn and its neighbour, Harvard House, are perhaps the finest timber-framed buildings in Stratford. Harvard House, built in 1596, was the home of Thomas Rogers, an alderman of Stratford, whose daughter, Katherine, married Southwark innkeeper Robert Harvard in 1605. By this time, Shakespeare had bought a splendid house for his retirement just along the street. We can easily imagine that the Rogers, the Harvards and the Shakespeares were well acquainted, and that Will Shakespeare often stepped across this threshold and looked out through these very windows. Katherine and Robert's son, John, sailed to America, but died in Boston a year after he arrived. He left half of his estate to the 'erecting of a college' and specified that 'all his library', 400 volumes, should be kept there. Harvard House is now owned by Harvard University.

Next to the Garrick, on the corner of Ely Street, is the Tudor House. This was the residence of the wealthy and influential Woolmer family from the reign of Elizabeth I until that of George II. The lowest storey has an entirely modern shop-front, but at the corner there is the projecting end of the dragon (or diagonal) beam with carvings of a quasi-Ionic capital, some ornament and a human mask. Above this are a couple of wonderful gargoyle-like carved wooden figures that few people notice. Across the street, many small reliefs of Shakespeare plays decorate the red-brick bank – you might have fun identifying them.

In Chapel Street, which is a continuation of High Street, and adjacent to the Town Hall, a very fine range of sixteenth-century buildings has been incorporated into the Shakespeare Hotel. Apparently, David Garrick suggested the rooms be named after Shakespeare's plays. At 4s 6d (23p) a night this was the most expensive hotel in the whole of Stratford at the beginning of the sixteenth century.

Farther along Chapel Street, you come to the site of New Place, once the grandest house in Stratford, which Shakespeare bought with his playhouse profits in May

1597. New Place was pulled down in 1759 by its disgruntled owner, the Reverend Gastrell, after a row with the civic authorities, but its foundations are currently being exhaustively investigated by a team of archaeologists.

Just next door is the house that once belonged to Thomas Nash, who married Shakespeare's granddaughter, Elizabeth. When Nash died, Elizabeth married John Barnard. Both marriages were childless, so Elizabeth was, sadly, Shakespeare's last descendant. The gardens are splendid, and in summer you can pick mulberries from Shakespeare's own mulberry tree. In truth, this tree is grown from a cutting, the original having been cut down in a fit of rage by the iconoclastic cleric Francis Gastrell, who was forced to quit the town 'amidst the rage and curses of its inhabitants'. Multifarious artefacts made from the tree's wood and subsequently sold as 'carved from Shakespeare's mulberry tree' could, apparently, only have been supplied by the felling of a small forest!

Shakespeare died at New Place in 1616, allegedly after a night of heavy drinking with fellow playwright Ben Jonson and the poet Michael Drayton. It might be that William was in no condition to over-indulge. His last will, made in the previous month, bears a shaky signature. Alterations to the will were made by Shakespeare in order to cross out his 'son-in-lawe' Thomas Quiney as a beneficiary, and substitute his daughter Judith's name. Judith had married local vintner Thomas Quiney at the distinctly shelvable age of thirty-one, and within two months, Quiney was to confess in open court to 'carnal copulation' with a local woman. Shakespeare was clearly determined that the dodgy Thomas Quiney was not going to benefit in the event of his death.

Opposite the site of New Place is the richly timbered sixteenth-century Falcon Inn, where the oldest Shakespeare society in the world, the Shakespeare Club, was founded in 1824. It was a two-storey private house when Shakespeare would have been able to see it from his parlour window. An extra storey was added in the seventeenth century. The Falcon has held a licence since the 1640s, longer than any other hostelry in the town.

Across the side street is the Guild Chapel, a fifteenth-century Decorated Gothic church, built for the Guild of the Holy Cross. Adjoining it is the handsome close-studded building of the Guild Hall. The upper hall accommodated a school, which was founded at least as early as 1555, and it has been used as a schoolroom continuously ever since. It is likely that Shakespeare received the learning that Ben Jonson dismissed as 'small Latin and less Greek' in this very building. He also very likely came to the Guild Hall with his father to watch performances by the Earl of Worcester's players, the Queen's Men and the Earl of Leicester's company. It is transporting to imagine him, barely five years old, sitting between his father's legs, watching the impossibly romantic players in wide-eyed wonder. You can usually visit this most atmospheric schoolroom on public holidays between 1 p.m. and 4 p.m. It is well worth the entrance fee of £2 to see the room to which, at seven in the morning in winter and six in summer, some forty of Shakespeare's contemporaries unwillingly crept with their satchels.

Then we come to the almshouses, built around 1427 to provide homes for aged townspeople. The tall brick chimneys are designed to carry the sparks well away from the roofs – thatched in those days. That puts us in mind of the devastation that William Shakespeare must have felt when he received the news in his house nearby that his beloved Globe Theatre, in Southwark, had burned down after a spark had ignited its thatch.

Opposite the Guild Hall and almshouses is certainly the best place to stay in Stratford and one of the best places to eat – the Church Street Town House. Shall we pop in for lunch? The rear of the house is seventeenth century, while the rooms at the front of the building were added in 1768. The ceiling light in the Red Dining Room is 200 years old, as is the beautiful oak staircase, which has a roof lantern to light it. At some point the facade underwent a fashionable facelift. The top of the building is castellated and ogée arches adorn the windows, making an interesting addition to the eclectic mix of architecture in the town.

After visiting the Town House, we'll walk to the church, following the route taken by Shakespeare's funeral cortege. Continue along what is now Church Street, past the civic offices and the Shakespeare Institute, until opposite an old Flower's pub, the Windmill, we come to a handsome, seven-bay, brick, Georgian townhouse, Mason Croft. This was the home of Marie Corelli, a flamboyant and popular writer of women's fiction, who sold more books in her time than Conan Doyle, H. G. Wells and Rudyard Kipling combined. Her special appeal to her female readers can be gauged from her response to an interviewer who asked why she had never married: 'I have three pets at home which answer the same purpose as a husband. I have a dog that growls every morning, a parrot that swears all afternoon, and a cat that comes home late at night.'

A review in the *Spectator* described her as 'a woman of deplorable talent who imagined that she was a genius, and she was accepted as a genius by a public whose commonplace sentimentalities and prejudices she gave a glamorous setting'. Marie's controversial ego was clearly in evidence when she imported a gondola, complete with gondolier, from Venice in which to disport herself up and down the river. We have cause to thank her today, though, because her determination to preserve the town's sixteenth- and seventeenth-century heritage led to the excrescences of later years being removed from some of the finest timber-framed buildings in its streets. In many instances, she paid for the restoration herself.

At the junction, we'll turn down Old Town – so called because it was the centre of the original town before the Bishop of Worcester's planned new town in 1196. A short way down the street, on the left, you will see Hall's Croft, a fine, timbered house with steeply pitched gables where Shakespeare's daughter Suzanna and her husband Dr John Hall lived. It's done out in the very latest Jacobean interior design, and Dr Hall's dispensary contains an exhibition of the rather worrying medical practices of the time. The magnificent garden includes a herbaceous border of old English flowers and a stately row of poplars.

159

And so, continuing down an avenue of lime trees, we come to Holy Trinity church. It's a beautiful late Gothic building with an elegant slender spire and a fine carillon of bells, which you may be lucky enough to hear ringing out across the town. Some fine thirteenth-century early English work can be seen in the aisles and transepts.

The knocker on the porch door is an old sanctuary ring – anyone escaping from the law could use it to seek thirty-seven days refuge, during which they might endeavour to reform and seek atonement. The practice was abolished in 1623. There is a fine set of misericords (upturned seats on which a weary worshipper may perch his bottom) in the choir with the customary folksy carvings – they are well worth detailed study. Look out for the mermaid combing her hair, a lecherous naked woman riding a stag, and an amusing depiction of marital disharmony – perhaps the woodcarver revenging himself upon his spouse. A wife is pulling her husband's beard and bashing him with a frying pan. Most bizarre of all is the carving of two rampant bears flanked by apes, one of which is providing a urine sample for the other!

The church marks the beginning and end of our great poet's life, for the font at which he was baptised is here and in the chancel of the church you will find his somewhat podgy bust, looking less like a passionate poet and more like a jolly burgher – which, of course, he probably was by the time he died. The bust has, in its time, fallen off its perch, and its damaged cheeks have been repaired, whitewashed and repainted, and its moustache remodelled a la mode!

As for the epitaph with its enigmatic appeal not to disturb the grave – 'Good frend for Jesus sake forbeare / To digg the dust enclosed heare / Blest be ye man yt spares thes stones and/Curst be he yt moves my bones' – he most probably didn't write what was simply a request to a future sexton not to remove his bones to the charnel house in order to make room for another dead soul. No mystery in that, really.

It's a pleasant walk along the river back to the Stratford Basin, and I can't think of a better way to finish our little outing together than by adjourning to the actors' pub on Waterside. The pub is actually called the Black Swan, but so many people got lost looking for the 'Dirty Duck', as it had been dubbed by generations of actors, that the sign outside has been repainted to include both names, one on each side. Perhaps people should be told they'll find the pub halfway from Cambridge to Bristol – you'll have to look about you to work that one out!

As we raise our glasses, let me suggest that if you have more time to spend in the area, you take a drive to Chipping Camden tomorrow, and bask in the honeyed gorgeousness of one of the most beautiful Cotswold villages. Do take a look in the silversmith's workshop in Sheep Street, where four generations of the same family have been making beautiful objects since 1888 when Charles Ashbee moved fifty craftsmen to this Utopian Arts & Crafts haven from their workshops in the East End of London.

If you prefer the idea of a ramble, Guiting Power is a good starting point. This wonderfully unspoilt village is about forty-five minutes' drive from Stratford, through Moreton-in-Marsh and Stow. Invest in an OS map and plan a circular walk, mostly using footpaths, to Naunton and back. You could fortify yourself with coffee and cake at the Old Post Office first, then arrive in the Black Horse Inn in Naunton in time for lunch.

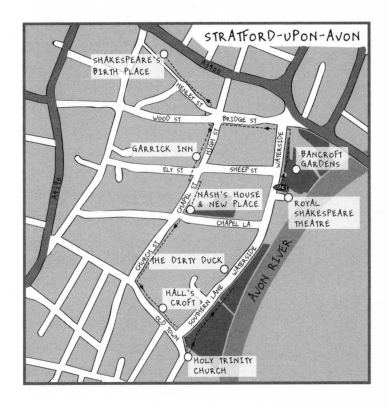

CHARTWELL –
THE GREAT ESCAPE

GILLIAN CHADWICK

'A day away from Chartwell is a day wasted.'
SIR WINSTON CHURCHILL

The house that became Sir Winston and Clementine
Churchill's family home for forty years is owned
today by the National Trust, which has preserved it as a
memorial to the man who led the people of Britain
through the Second World War. Chartwell is something
of a shrine to the man chosen by the public as the
Greatest Ever Briton, and thousands of visitors from
around the world come to share a little of the joy that
this property gave to Churchill during his lifetime.

As soon as Sir Winston set eyes on the place in 1921,
he was determined to make it his country retreat. The
house itself was not what attracted him, being a fairly

ordinary Victorian property constructed around a Tudor core. It was also in very poor condition and would obviously need a great deal of work (and money!) to make it into a suitable family home – he and his wife had four young children. What appealed to Sir Winston was the house's location, situated on a ridge and commanding magnificent views across the fields and woodlands of the Weald of Kent.

At this stage in his career, Churchill was member of parliament for Dundee, and Colonial Secretary in the Liberal government. Although he was supplementing his political salary with earnings from his considerable skills as an author, he was by no means a wealthy man, so with a wife and four young children to support, the asking price of £6,500 for the house with 32 hectares (80 acres) of land was unaffordable. The property remained on the market for one year and eventually the vendors accepted Churchill's offer of £5,000.

Unfortunately, at about the same time in 1922, Sir Winston lost his seat in parliament and so was faced with the costs of restoring and converting the property without his parliamentary income. The original estimate for the works was £7,000. In 1924, when the house was finally ready to move into, the final amount spent had soared to over £18,000! No wonder Clementine was unimpressed with this huge outlay and always said that they really could not afford Chartwell. They were always short of money and Sir Winston had to write constantly in order to pay the bills.

While the work on the house was under way, the family spent some of their time in a rented villa in the South of France where Sir Winston could continue writing his book, *The World Crisis*, which was a history of the First World War. They also rented Hosey Rigge, which was soon nicknamed Cosy Pig, a house on nearby Hosey Hill. This house was owned by Alice Liddell, for whom Charles Dodgson, better known as Lewis Carroll, had written the Alice in Wonderland stories when she was a little girl living in Oxford. Her father was dean of Christ Church College, where Charles Dodgson was a professor of mathematics.

Churchill's financial situation improved somewhat in 1924 when, having left the Liberal Party, he was re-elected to parliament as a Conservative and became Chancellor of the Exchequer. Naturally, most of his work was London based but he still spent as much time as he could at his new country home, and continued to do so at every possible opportunity during the next forty years until his death in 1965. It was only here at Chartwell, surrounded by their adored children, grandchildren and pets, that he and Clementine could totally relax.

In 1929, Churchill's fortunes took a downturn when the Labour Party was voted into power. He lost his position as Chancellor of the Exchequer and, to make matters much worse, he lost a great deal of his invested literary earnings during the Wall Street crash. He retained his parliamentary seat but disagreed with his party and the government over their concessions to Indian independence. His opinions on India were not popular and his reputation and political influence suffered.

During the next ten years, the so-called 'wilderness years', while he was isolated from the centre of politics, Sir Winston worked assiduously on several books, including his autobiography, the story of his life until 1908, the year of his marriage to Clementine, and a biography of his ancestor, Sir John Churchill, the Duke of Marlborough. These, together with the income from his newspaper articles, kept the wolf from the door and enabled him to devote a great deal of time to improving the grounds of the property.

He enlarged the existing lakes, installed a swimming pool and created a water garden, filling a series of pools with exotic goldfish. Clementine planned the layout and the planting of the fragrant Rose Garden, which lies between the Water Garden and the main house. The old tennis court on the other side of the house became a croquet lawn, providing hours of fun for family and friends during the summer months.

Here, by the path to the croquet lawn, the visitor finds the graves of Rufus, Sir Winston's favourite poodle, and Jock his marmalade cat. A confirmed lover of all living things, Churchill derived great pleasure from feeding the fish in the ponds and the black swans on the lake. He also particularly liked pigs, saying, 'Dogs look up to us. Cats look down on us. Pigs treat us as equals.' His insistence on growing buddleia and ice plants was so that he could enjoy the spectacle of butterflies clustering around their favourite flowers.

During the early part of this period, Churchill embarked upon his do-it-yourself building projects, among them Marycote, which is a little summerhouse that he constructed for his youngest daughter, Mary, and the wall surrounding the kitchen garden. This was no small task since the wall is about 2.5 metres (8 feet) high and stands on a hill. He did most of the bricklaying himself. His chickens were not left out – he built them a brand new henhouse, which he named Chickenham Palace!

Probably Sir Winston's favourite way of relaxing was to be ensconced, paintbrush in hand, in his studio at the bottom of the garden, where he could while away the hours at his easel. His enthusiasm for painting knew no bounds, helping him to cope with the innumerable stresses and strains of his daily life, and during his lifetime he produced over 500 paintings. Many of these decorate the walls in the main house and many more canvases can be seen still displayed in his studio.

In the early 1930s, Churchill began to voice concerns that Hitler was secretly rearming and rebuilding the German army, and warned against the British government's policy of appeasement. He felt that Britain should increase its military strength rather than continue with its disarmament policies, but his opponents saw him as a warmonger. Eventually, he was able to persuade the government to heed his warnings, acknowledge the increasing German rearmament and take preventative action. These events are related in the 2002 film *The Gathering Storm*, the title taken from the first volume of Churchill's six-volume history of the Second World War. The film starred Albert Finney as Sir Winston and Vanessa Redgrave as Clementine, and much of it was filmed on location at Chartwell.

As events in Europe steadily worsened with the annexation of Austria and the invasion of Czechoslovakia, Poland appeared to be next on Hitler's agenda. Churchill was at Chartwell on 1 September 1939 when he heard the news that Poland had been attacked. He was called to London and Prime Minister Chamberlain appointed him as First Lord of the Admiralty, the position he had held during the First World War. Britain and France declared war on Germany on 3 September 1939. Eight months later, on the same day that Germany invaded France and the Low Countries, Churchill took over from Chamberlain as prime minister. His own words describe his feelings at this time: 'I felt as if I were walking with destiny and all my past life had been in preparation for this hour and this trial.'

It was clear that most of his time would now be taken up directing the War Cabinet from 10 Downing Street and the nearby Cabinet War Rooms, the secret underground bunker connected by tunnels to Downing Street. He also had the use of Chequers, the country residence given to the nation by Lord and Lady Lee of Fareham after the First World War, for all future prime ministers to use for rest and recreation. It was therefore decided to close down the main house at Chartwell for the duration of the war. The Churchills still managed to come down for a few weekends, when they stayed in Orchard Cottage, one of the smaller cottages near the studio at the bottom of the garden.

One of the deciding factors in closing Chartwell was security. Its position in Kent was directly under 'Bomb Alley', the flight path taken by the Luftwaffe *en route* to their bombing raids on London during the Blitz. The house and estate were particularly conspicuous due to the layout of lakes and pools surrounded by lawns in an otherwise mainly tree-covered landscape. Certain measures were taken to disguise these areas, especially the distinctive water garden, which had to be somehow covered up. Sir Winston was very concerned about the welfare of his beloved fish, and great care was taken in preventing them from coming to any harm during the camouflage work.

After victory in Europe was achieved on 8 May 1945, a general election was called, despite Churchill's wishes to delay an election until after Japan had been defeated. Thanks to his inspirational leadership during the war, Churchill was at the height of his popularity, but this did not help when it came to the country's choice of political party to lead post-war Britain. The election took place on 5 July and Churchill was devastated when the Labour party gained a clear majority and Clement Attlee,

Churchill's deputy in the coalition government during the war, took over as prime minister.

With Japan's surrender on 14 August 1945, the Second World War was over. Dejected, disappointed and exhausted, Sir Winston decided to recharge his batteries by taking a long holiday in Italy and the South of France, where he could paint to his heart's content during the sunshine-filled days. When he returned in 1946, he was once again in financial difficulty and made the heartbreaking decision to put his beloved Chartwell on the market. At this point, one of Sir Winston's greatest friends stepped in with an extremely generous offer. Lord Camrose, together with sixteen other friends, raised the £50,000 needed to purchase Chartwell and gave the property to the National Trust, on the condition that Sir Winston and Clementine could live there for the rest of their lives.

In the 1951 general election, the Conservative Party regained power and, at seventy-seven years of age, Churchill became prime minister for the second time. His workload was huge. He was responsible not only for home affairs but was also greatly involved in trying to improve relations between the United States and Russia during the Cold War period. His health suffered and he had a serious stroke in 1953. There were calls for his resignation but his subsequent recovery, and stubborn determination, enabled him to continue as prime minister until 1955.

His writing career had continued unabated since the end of the war. Chief among his output was his six-volume history of the Second World War, written mainly in his study at Chartwell between 1948 and 1951. In 1953, he was awarded the Nobel prize for literature for his contributions in the fields of history and biography, as well as for his mastery of the English language, which he so powerfully demonstrated in his magnificent speeches. His output continued undiminished, and he completed the four-volume *History of the English Speaking Peoples* when he was well into his eighties.

In 1958, the Churchills celebrated their fiftieth wedding anniversary. Sir Winston clearly adored Clementine, stating once that his most brilliant achievement was 'to persuade my wife to marry me'. On another occasion, at a dinner party, he was asked what he would like to be, if he could not be himself. His reply was, 'If I could not be who I am, I would most like to be ... Mrs Churchill's second husband.'

As a very special golden anniversary present, the four surviving Churchill children (one daughter, Marigold, had died at the age of two) had the Golden Rose Garden planted at Chartwell. It is still a delight, over sixty years later, to stroll among this sea of golden and yellow roses and inhale their delicious scents. Watercolour paintings of these roses can be seen in the *Golden Rose Book*, on permanent display in the dining room. The paintings are by famous artists of the time, including Augustus John, Duncan Grant and John Nash, who were commissioned by the Churchill children to create this unique and precious gift.

During his long and illustrious career, Churchill was showered with countless awards and gifts by his admirers from all over the world. Three former bedrooms in the house have been converted into a museum, so visitors are able to see a selection of these on display, together with some of his uniforms and decorations. One of his proudest moments was being invested by the young Elizabeth II as a Knight of the Order of the Garter in 1953, and thereby becoming a member of the highest order of chivalry in this country. His robes, banner and insignia are displayed quite close to the record of another honour, also a source of great pride, the certificate proclaiming Sir Winston Churchill an honorary citizen of the United States of America, awarded to him by President J.F. Kennedy in 1963.

In the adjoining study, the visitor most feels the lingering presence of the great man. This was his favourite room, where he spent so much of his time during his forty years at Chartwell. It is full of personal objects, including portraits of his family perched on the large mahogany desk that belonged to his father, together with his cigar cutter and spectacles, and little busts of Nelson and Napoleon, whom he greatly admired.

Decorating the walls are portraits of his parents – a painting of his father, Lord Randolph, depicted in his robes as Chancellor of the Exchequer, and a charcoal portrait by John Singer Sargent of his beautiful mother Jennie, of whom he said, 'She shone for me like the evening star. I loved her dearly, but at a distance.' As was the custom in upper-class families at the time, his early years were spent mainly in the care of his nanny, and then at boarding schools, so he did not get much attention from his parents.

Several flags are displayed in the study, one of which used to fly from the flagpole on the roof, announcing that Sir Winston was in residence. This was his Lord Warden of the Cinque Ports standard, and on his death it was flown at half mast. The Union Flag over the fireplace was hoisted in Rome on the night of 4 June

1944, the first allied flag to be hoisted over a liberated European capital. The Knight of the Order of the Garter banner, which used to hang above his stall at St George's Chapel, Windsor, is also displayed in this room.

A present from the Shah of Persia lies on the floor of the study – a beautiful carpet that Sir Winston ruined one night when he became so fed up with tripping over the border tassles that he snipped them all off with a pair of nail scissors! Two more charming gifts are the little soft toys given to Sir Winston by some factory workers. They can still be seen on the study bookshelves, where he used them to mark the places where he had removed books, so he knew where to put them back.

Towards the end of his life Sir Winston spent more of his time in sunnier climes, usually in the South of France, but he and Lady Churchill still returned frequently to Chartwell. In October 1964, when Sir Winston was in very poor health, they moved to their home in London. He had stated many years previously that he was ready to meet his maker, 'But whether my Maker is prepared for the great ordeal of meeting me is another matter.' On the seventieth anniversary of his father's death, 24 January 1965, surrounded by his family and with his ginger cat at his side, the great man passed away, and the nation went into a state of deep mourning.

An indication of how much Churchill had loved Chartwell was that he had once told his family that he would like to be buried there. However, he had a change of mind and decided he would prefer to be buried beside his parents and brother in the graveyard of St Martin's Church, Bladon, just a short distance from Blenheim Palace, where he had been born ninety years earlier.

Lady Churchill did not wish to remain at Chartwell after Sir Winston's death, so the property was handed over in full to the National Trust and they continue to look after this marvellously evocative place on behalf of the nation.

CONSTABLE COUNTRY AND COLCHESTER – PAINTED LANDSCAPE

HILARY RATCLIFFE

This trip is a real treat for a day out, and a day of contrasts – quintessential English countryside immortalised by John Constable together with the story of a dauntless Celtic tribal leader sacking three Roman towns. So first the landscape.

From London through rural Essex and into Suffolk you cross over the River Stour – pronounced as in 'dour'. The river was canalised by act of parliament in 1705 and wends its way 26 miles from Sudbury to Brantham sea lock. In the old days, products such as oil, pitch, coal, sugar, grindstones, wheat and barley were transported along it, and the bricks that were used to build the Albert Hall in London. The goods were carried in lighters, a kind of flat-bottomed barge pulled by a horse, known locally as the Suffolk Punch. Boats and horses are immortalised in Constable's paintings, such as *Flatford Mill, scenes on a navigable river* in the Victoria & Albert Museum in London and *The White Horse* in the Frick Museum in New York.

Once over the Stour, we are in Suffolk and the countryside beloved by Constable, which gave him his inspiration. He said of this area: 'I should paint my own places best ... I associate my careless boyhood with all that lies on the banks of the Stour.'

Constable was born in East Bergholt, son of Golding and Ann Constable. His father owned the mills at Dedham, Flatford and Langham. After inheriting money from his father, John Constable married Maria, the granddaughter of the rector of East Bergholt – once moneyed, he was seen as a suitable husband.

The bell tower of East Bergholt church remains half-finished. Its construction was being paid for by Cardinal Wolsey, and when he fell from grace, having failed to secure a divorce for Henry VIII, he was arrested, and money for his ecclesiastical projects dried up. And so today, the church's bells are housed in a wooden cage in the churchyard and are rung by hand – unique.

These days, Flatford Mill is owned by the National Trust. They try to keep the surrounding landscape much as it was in Constable's time and so you are able to work out exactly where many of his famous paintings are set. The way down to the river is through a wooded vale, at the bottom of which is a beautiful wildlife garden, planted and looked after by the Royal Society for the Protection of Birds. Two small thatched cottages from Constable's day now house the NT visitor centre.

Cross over the bridge – a replica paid for by another famous painter from the area, Alfred Munnings. Now we are at the spot on the river exactly where Constable painted his scenes of the Suffolk Punch pulling the lighters. Constable had a special trick to attract the viewer's focus, namely the use of red. In this case, the colour is used on the horse's noseband.

Walking along beside the river, you will come to a lock, a modern paddle design replacement for the original one of Constable's time (which can be seen alongside). The old locks were wasteful of water and so were replaced. Carry on and you will come to the site of *The White Horse*. Look across the river for a view of Willy Lott's cottage. Constable's picture of this scene shows a horse actually on a lighter. At the time, the river at this point was tidal and the horse is being given a ride using the tidal flow. Downriver, it would have stepped off on to the towpath on the opposite bank and continued to tow the lighter to Brantham lock.

Cross over to the other side of the river to the tea room. No remains were known of the building depicted in Constable's painting *Boat building on the Stour* until the tea room was being built in the 1980s, when lo and behold, a dry dock was discovered, which established where the boat building in the painting had taken place.

Continuing past the granary where John's father Golding kept his grain, you come to a beautiful timber-framed, wattle and daub fourteenth-century farmhouse, and then to Flatford Mill itself. In this part of England there is little stone, so the old houses are a combination of timber frame, wattle and daub and brick. In places, knapped flint was used, usually in churches, for example Stratford St Mary. The houses are often painted in what is known as Suffolk pink. This might be purchased today from exclusive paint manufacturers but in the past it was a limewash coloured with pig's blood!

Flatford Mill was a working mill until the early twentieth century. Today, it is used as a field studies centre. Right here is the flat ford and this is the site of *The Haywain*, perhaps the best loved of John Constable's work. The cart in the middle of the flat ford in the painting is probably one that carries logs rather than a haywain. The horses are pulling it across the flat ford formed by the water after it has flowed through the mill and mill race and where this flow has created a hard surface. What is happening is not exactly clear, but does that matter? It was a perfect excuse for the artist to portray his beloved river: 'The sound of water escaping from mill dams, willows, old rotten planks, slimy posts and brickwork. I love such things.'

On to Dedham, where Constable walked across the fields to school. Here there are interesting American connections. In the seventeenth century, many people from this village, intent on the religious freedom denied them here, joined the *Mayflower* for its voyage to America. There they helped establish colonies on the eastern seaboard of what would become the United States. As a result, there is a Dedham in Massachusetts and the badge of that town is on display in the beautiful church here in the English Dedham. Also, you will find, on the back pew, carvings depicting some of the flora and fauna to be found in Massachusetts.

The church has two memorials, one to Judith Eyre who died from accidentally swallowing a pin, and the other to a family called Sherman who left for America. Their initials may be seen in a window. One of the family's descendants was the Major William Sherman who marched through Georgia during the American Civil War. What astonishing things you can find in a country church if you look carefully.

Now our journey takes us away from the countryside and back into Colchester, or Camulodunum as the Romans called it. This was the first recorded town in Britain, noted by Pliny in AD 77, but its history goes back way before that. This was the headquarters of the Catevellauni tribe.

The Roman story begins with the Roman emperor Claudius and his pursuit of glory. What better way to achieve this, he thought, than to conquer the rebellious British? And there were good reasons to undertake this conquest. The Britons were only too willing to help out the rebellious Gauls – every time the Romans tried to defeat the Gauls, they simply escaped across the Channel! – and the country was a rich source of lead, tin, gold, hunting dogs and slaves. And part of the reason the Romans came to Colchester was that it was, and is, the centre for some of the finest oysters in this country. The Romans liked oysters. Colchester still has an oyster festival.

The perfect opportunity for the Romans presented itself when in AD 40 the tribal leader Cunobellin died.

He had three sons. Caractacus and Todgodumnus rebelled against the Romans, and one, Adminius, was prepared to be a client king and accept Roman rule. Claudius sent his favoured Roman general Aulus Plautius with 40,000 men and defeat was, shall we say, inevitable. The triumphal procession was delayed for sixteen weeks to allow Claudius himself to come to Britain, and to parade not only with his legions but also with elephants! You can't help but wonder what on earth the Celtic Britons made of that.

For five years, until AD 49, Camulodunum was the capital of Britain. After that, it was Londinium's (London's) turn.

The next stage in Colchester's story starts in AD 60 when the Romans attempted to 'assimilate' the neighbouring tribe of the Iceni. The Iceni were led by King Prasugatus, who was killed in the ensuing fighting. His wife was beaten and his daughters raped. Here an indomitable heroine takes over the story, because his wife was Boudicca and she wasn't having it. Raising the tribes of the Iceni and the Trinovantes, Boudicca marched on Camoludunum. The supporters of Rome fled to the temple built by Claudius, whereupon Boudicca set it on fire. She then marched on London, sacked the city and turned her attention to Verulamium, modern-day

St Albans. She burned that as well and prepared to meet the hastily summoned legions, who were hotfooting it back from North Wales. Somewhere, probably in Bedfordshire, battle was joined and Boudicca was defeated. According to the Roman historian Tacitus, rather than be taken to Rome as a prisoner, Boudicca swallowed poison on the battlefield and died.

Britain's warrior queen has been immortalised in stories, television programmes and, best of all, in a very Victorian statue at the north side of Westminster Bridge, the original heroine who resisted domination by an invading foe. Next to the Parliament buildings is a suitable place for a statue celebrating resistance to authority, wouldn't you say?

So what is left of this great Roman story in Colchester? Well, underneath the Norman castle are the foundations of the Claudian temple; the city has the best-preserved Roman city walls in England, and many artefacts from the time can be seen in the Castle Museum. And there's a special chapel – St Helen's chapel – whereby hangs another tale.

St Helen, or Helena as she is also known, was, according to legend, the daughter of Old King Cole, that merry old soul of nursery rhyme fame. He was a third-century king reputed to have built the early town of

Colchester and after whom it was named. The site of a Roman gravel pit in the town is still known as King Cole's Kitchen. Helen was born in Colchester and was the mother of Constantine the Great, the Roman emperor who declared in AD 313 that the Roman Empire was to be Christian.

As the patron saint of the town, a statue of St Helen resides on top of the town hall while Colchester's coat of arms reflects her life, spent in pursuit of holy relics – parts of the True Cross, that is the cross on which Christ was crucified, the three crowns worn by the Magi and the nails used to nail Christ to the cross. The town badge includes in its design those three crowns, nails and a cross.

Tradition has it that the chapel, which is near the castle, was built by Helen for her private use. It is certainly very old and made partly with Roman brick. In its time, the chapel has been many things, including a school, a library and a warehouse, but now it has been restored as a place of worship.

There is more to Colchester than its amazing Roman story. It also has what is known as the Dutch Quarter, the story of which goes back to the sixteenth century. At a time when all Europe was arguing over religion, the Netherlands was divided into Spanish Roman Catholic possessions in the south and the Protestant United Provinces in the North. When persecution of Protestants began, many fled to the nearest part of England – East Anglia and, in particular, Colchester. The refugees brought with them their skill at weaving – Colchester became famous for the light woollen cloths known as bays and says – and their distinctive architecture, hence the Dutch Quarter. Less happily, in the time of Mary Tudor (1553–58) when Protestants were being burnt at the stake as heretics, Colchester suffered more deaths that any other town in England apart from London.

So to the castle itself. Built by Eudo de Rie in the time of William the Conqueror, the design of its keep is the same as Rochester's castle and also the White Tower at the Tower of London, except that Colchester castle is much bigger. The reason is that the Normans decided to use the foundations of the original Roman temple of Claudius and build on to those. So underneath a Norman castle there is a Roman temple, which you can visit if you are good at scrambling through narrow spaces. How wonderful that it is still there.

The castle has been involved in two sieges. One took place after King John had signed and sealed Magna Carta at Runnymede and then tried to break his promises, the other during the Civil War in the seventeenth century. As you would expect, Colchester, being Puritan, sided with Parliament. However, during the latter part of the war, Royalists, led by Sir George Lisle and Sir Charles Lucas, took the town on behalf of the king. This led to a seventy-six-day siege during which the people of Colchester were unwillingly caught up in the fight between the Royalists and the Roundhead army led by Sir Thomas Fairfax. The townspeople were reduced to eating rats, cats and dogs. To rub salt into the wound, when eventually Fairfax won and Lisle and Lucas had been shot, the town was fined the equivalent of £2 million in today's money.

The castle was eventually sold to John Wheeley, an ironmonger, who in the late seventeenth century decided to blow it up and use it for building materials. However, the Normans and Romans were such good builders that he wasn't able to achieve this aim, and the castle continued life as a bit of a white elephant until 1726 when it was given to Charles Gray on the occasion of his wedding. His house, Hollytrees, was right next door – the castle was a kind of folly in his back garden! He adapted it, built on to the roof and had a library and study there, and so it remained until the twentieth century when money donated by the Member of Parliament for Colchester, Viscount Cowdray, was used to buy it and turn it into a museum for the town.

One recurring theme in the Colchester story has been elephants – both real and the white kind – and there remains one more story to tell that involves this beast, concerning a water tower built in the nineteenth century.

The local priest, who lived more or less under the shadow of the huge tower, christened it Jumbo, the name taken from an elephant that resided in London's zoo until 1882, when it was sold to Phineas Taylor Barnum, the circus owner and impresario. He took Jumbo on tour and, sadly, a few years later, Jumbo was in a collision with a freight train in Canada and came off worse. To safeguard his investment, Barnum had Jumbo stuffed and showed him like that. For many generations, children in England referred to any elephant as 'Jumbo'. The water tower that dominates the town is still called Jumbo.

So from elephants in a triumphal procession led by a Roman emperor to a water tower from the Victorian period, Colchester is a town of surprises.

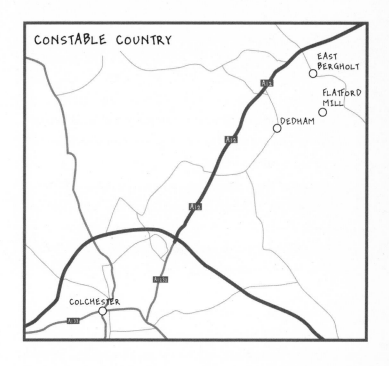

St Albans –
THE CITY THAT
CHANGED ITS NAME

ALISON HOOK

Saint Albans is a city full of firsts and superlatives. For one, it is named after England's first Christian martyr. Alban was a respected citizen, living in Verulamium at some time during the third century. The third largest city in Roman Britain, Verulamium was situated to the west of present-day St Albans, taking in part of Verulamium Park and some of the Gorhambury estate.

Legend has it that Alban was visited by a travelling Christian priest, Amphibalus, and as a result converted to Christianity. The Roman authorities were not happy about Amphibalus's presence in the city and issued a warrant for his arrest. Alban helped Amphibalus to escape by lending him his cloak to cover his face. The disguise was successful and Amphibalus was able to leave the city unharmed. Amphibalus is often referred to as Saint Overcoat as a result.

The day following the escape, Alban was called to the basilica to stand trial for his action and required to renounce his faith. The basilica, which was the equivalent of a central criminal court today, stood on the site of the present church of St Michaels and was next to the forum (town hall and public market place), which was where the Roman museum now stands. Alban repeatedly refused to renounce his faith and was eventually sentenced to death.

The Romans never performed executions or buried the dead within their city walls. According to Matthew Paris, a monk writing in the thirteenth century, Alban was led from one of the gates (near where the Fighting Cocks pub stands today) and taken to the top of Holywell Hill, the site of the present abbey church and cathedral. It is said that the waters of the River Ver parted and fresh water springs appeared on the hillside in order to ease Alban's journey and in response to his treatment – the reason why Holywell Hill became so named. In addition, red roses bloomed, the explanation for why, in art, St Alban is always depicted holding a red rose.

At the top of the hill, Alban was tied to a tree but the executioner, a soldier, refused to carry out the task and a second had to be found. Finding a more willing executioner was made easier as the first was killed for failing to carry out an order. Allegedly, when Alban's head fell to the ground, the eyes of the second executioner popped out, such was his shame and disgust for the act that he had committed.

News of this act of barbarism circulated around the country and Alban's burial place soon became a shrine where miracles were said to occur, and pilgrims travelled there to pay their respects.

Every year on the Saturday nearest Saint Alban's day, 22 June, a re-enactment of Alban's trial and martyrdom takes place, using huge puppets to represent the key players in the story. It is a colourful spectacle that includes the executioner's giant eyeballs, which roll down the hill after the puppet of Alban is felled. The pageant is followed by a service in the cathedral and everyone is given a red rose in memory of the saint. Many people think that, as the first Christian martyr in this country, Alban and his red rose should replace George and his dragon as England's patron saint.

The Romans left Britain in AD 410 when they were recalled to Rome to defend their own country from attack. Gradually, Verulamium fell into decline, but sufficient of its Roman origins survived to be discovered in excavations. Today, in Verulamium Park, you can see the outline of the London Gate, one of the gates that led into the city, and a small part of the Roman wall that surrounded and protected the city. The modern, purpose-built Hypocaust building in the park houses one of the finest mosaic floors to be discovered in Britain – plus a hypocaust, a system of underfloor heating. Nothing is new!

The museum in St Albans was established in the 1930s following the excavations conducted by Mortimer

Wheeler and his wife Tessa. It is noted for its large colourful mosaics and its wealth of everyday and ceremonial artefacts, such as pottery (Samian ware), amphora, jewellery, coins, tools, grave goods, games and all the paraphernalia associated with bathing – the Romans were very fond of their baths. There is also the coffin and perfectly preserved remains of a Roman male, who is affectionately known as Posthumus. This is one of the best Roman museums in Britain and should not be missed.

After the Romans departed, the city came under the jurisdiction of the kings of Mercia. The story goes that in 793, King Offa of Mercia had a dream in which he was instructed to endow a Benedictine monastery that stood on the site of Alban's martyrdom. From then until its dissolution in 1539, Saint Albans Abbey was the premier abbey in Britain, and was visited by all the kings and queens of England. Little remains of the abbey (a monastery under the rule of an abbot) today, but you can still see the magnificent Abbey Gateway. This stands next to the west entrance of the present cathedral, which is officially known as the Cathedral and Abbey Church of Saint Alban.

The gateway is now part of Saint Albans School but it was once the private entrance of the abbot, who was responsible for the everyday running of the monastery and its guests. The present gateway was built in 1362 after an earlier structure had been destroyed by a particularly violent storm. When you stand in front of the gateway, notice the particularly fine castellation. A law of the time decreed that buildings could only be castellated with the permission of the monarch, so the castellation on the gateway is a clear sign that the abbey had received the royal seal of approval.

Going through the gateway, you would have entered the monastery at its north-west corner; and on the south side wall of the cathedral nave (the longest nave in England), the outline of the cloisters can be clearly seen. The cloisters would have led to the domestic buildings of the monastery. These would have included a chapter house, dining room, dormitory, hospital and the scriptorium in which Matthew Paris wrote the story of Alban's execution. The cloisters provided the link between the spiritual world of the church and the domestic life of the monastery.

The monks were a well-organised, self-sufficient community, growing their own produce, brewing their own ale and making their own wine. Today, their way of life is remembered in the street names around the abbey, for example Orchard Street, Fishpool Street and the Vintry Gardens.

The monks also ran a school for sons of the wealthy and aristocratic families of Hertfordshire. Many of their pupils went on to enter life in the abbey, but one, Nicholas Breakspear, was rejected by the abbot. Determined to enter the church, Breakspear travelled to France where he joined the cloister of Saint Rufus near Arles. Clearly suited to his calling, and highly successful in it, he later became pope, the first and currently only Englishman ever to have held that position. He was elected Pope Adrian IV in 1154. Years later, he met the abbot who had refused to allow him to join the St Albans monastery, and when he questioned him about that decision, the abbot very cleverly replied, 'I knew you were destined for greater things.'

A further claim to fame is that discussions on the first draft of Magna Carta took place in the abbey's chapter house before the charter was returned to Westminster.

As the fame of Alban's shrine grew, the tenth-century Abbot Ulsinus came to realise that pilgrims and tourists visiting the shrine were bypassing Verulamium, and that the town's inhabitants were missing out on some potential spending power. He therefore encouraged the people living in Verulamium to move up the hill and build new homes in what is the centre of the present town. As an incentive, he allowed the townspeople reduced rates and even free rights to trade in the market.

Ulsinus changed the layout of the city by establishing three churches to mark its boundaries – Saint Michael's, Saint Stephen's and Saint Peter's. After this, visitors began to refer to the city as Saint Albans, after the shrine they were visiting.

The market has always been a focal point of the city and is the oldest street market in England. It received its official charter from Edward VI in 1553 but a market had existed here as early as the ninth century. A good time to visit St Albans is on a Wednesday or Saturday when the street market is held. Additionally, a farmer's market is held on the second Sunday of every month.

Until its dissolution, the abbey was responsible for the everyday running of the town, and it was to the abbot that taxes were paid. Relations between the townsfolk and the abbey were not always cordial. When the Peasants' Revolt broke out in London in 1381, a group of men from St Albans went to the capital to offer their services. They were advised to return home and lead their own revolt. Back in St Albans, the men stormed the abbey only to discover that the abbot had taken hold of his skirts and fled. His house was ransacked in his absence and the querns (vessels in which cereal was ground) removed from the floor. The abbot had taken these from the townspeople so that he could charge for their use.

Later, when he returned, the cowardly abbot promised to meet the demands of the people, which were to reinstate the ancient laws of liberty and freedom. The peace did not last long, however. After quelling the revolt in London, Richard II rode to St Albans to arrest and try the ringleaders. They were found guilty and hanged, drawn and quartered outside the city. One of the protesters, John Ball, a Christian priest, expressed his disgust at the inequality in society by coining a phrase that is still in use today: 'When Adam delved and Eve span, who was then the gentleman'.

Antagonism between 'town and gown' was also the motivation behind the building of the clock tower that stands just outside the abbey walls. Taxes were paid to the abbot. Whenever the pope or the king needed to supplement his finances, taxes were increased, and if they were not paid, the abbot would refuse to ring the curfew bell. The curfew bell was essential to the smooth running of the city because it told the townsfolk when to get up. A second bell was rung at night to tell them to put out their fires, and in a town made almost entirely of wood, this was no mean consideration.

Resentful of the power of the abbey, the townspeople raised money to build their own clock tower. This magnificent edifice was erected between 1403 and 1412, the only medieval, free-standing clock tower of its kind in England. Just so the monks were aware of how the citizens felt, it was built to stand higher than the abbey wall, enabling the town to overlook its rival. The clock tower is open in the summer and the view of Hertfordshire from the roof is well worth the climb up the steep spiral staircase.

It was near the clock tower that the first Battle of St Albans took place, and although little more than a skirmish, it heralded the start of the Wars of the Roses, a dynastic civil war that was to last for forty-five years and tear families apart.

St Albans Abbey was closed by Henry VIII and the land and building materials sold to wealthy aristocrats of the city. The abbey church, however, was allowed to remain, following a petition to the king by the townsfolk, who wanted to use it as their parish church. As a result, the church is today the oldest place of continuous Christian worship in Britain.

Today, the abbey church and cathedral are a patchwork of different building styles, illustrating how fashions change. The impressive tower dates from

Norman times. The Saxon construction was rebuilt by Abbot Paul of Caen in 1077. However, look carefully at the bricks and you will realise that they are in fact Roman tiles, which were looted from the old city of Verulamium – an early example of recycling.

Much of the present building dates from the Victorian period. It was restored following the collapse of part of the nave wall in 1832 and to a large extent rebuilt to the designs of Edmund Beckett, 1st Baron Grimthorpe. He was a wealthy citizen of the town, who put up the money for a competition to design and fund a new church. Grimthorpe was an amateur architect himself and so it comes as no surprise to learn that all of the designs submitted were lost except his and he won the competition.

By profession, Grimthorpe was a horologist and his claim to fame is that he designed the mechanism for the clock of the Palace of Westminster, which operates the chimes of Big Ben. He is responsible for much of the appearance of the cathedral today, particularly the west front, and its design caused much controversy at the time. Purists were horrified and took great objection to the mini turrets that appear on either side of the west front, referring to them as Grimthorpe's pepper pots. Such was the outcry that the Society for the Protection of Ancient Buildings was formed. However, time has changed our perceptions and today the west front, built of pale Ancaster stone, blends into its surroundings.

Grimthorpe had wanted to restore the building to its original proportions and this involved removing the wall between the main building and the Lady Chapel, where, since the Dissolution, a school had been held. Imagine his delight when, between the walls, he discovered the remains of Saint Alban's shrine. It had been smashed into pieces, but was painstakingly pieced together and can be visited today.

Inside the church, note the wonderful carved wooden watching loft, where the monks could observe the pilgrims to check that they did not help themselves to the offerings that had been left at the shrine. The newly restored church was given the status of a cathedral in 1877 and St Albans officially became a city. No visit to St Albans is complete without exploring this wonderful building.

In the eighteenth and nineteenth centuries, St Albans became the town where coaches would stop on their way to and from the capital, twenty miles' distant. In 1815, it was estimated that seventy mail and stage coaches passed through the town daily. The taverns and inns that had once housed pilgrims now offered hospitality to the drivers and passengers, and places to rest, water and feed the horses. Coaching inns can be seen throughout St Albans. One of the most striking of these stands at the top of George Street. Formerly the Tudor Tavern, this half-timbered building is typical of those built in the fourteenth century. The first floor juts out about 30 centimetres (a foot) further than the ground floor. In those days, you paid for the land your foundations stood on, so this was a way of getting more space for your money. The tavern's black and white appearance – often referred to as the magpie effect – is very much a Victorian affectation following the discovery of whitewash and a black oil-based paint. Originally, the building would have shown silvered oak beams with an infill of wattle and daub. Notice the enormous bowed oak beam, the result of building in green oak, which warps as it dries out.

The present city is a pleasing mix of medieval alleyways around the clock tower and wide tree-lined street around St Peters. This area was laid out when the old town hall was built. The old town hall is easily recognised. It is the white classical building that stands in the centre of the city. Built to the design of George Smith in 1831, it houses a perfectly preserved oak-panelled magistrates court and the old police holding cells. Prisoners were brought up from the cells to stand in the dock facing the magistrate. The chief magistrate was always the Lord Mayor of the city and one of the most well known of these was Samuel Ryder, who founded the Ryder Cup golf tournament. Samuel Ryder was Lord Mayor three times. He was a very well-respected nurseryman, who began his career selling packets of seeds from a wheelbarrow outside the post office. Today, his offices are occupied by the Comfort Hotel, and the spectacular art deco building next to it was his glass showroom where he exhibited his plants and sold his seeds. His interest in golf developed after his doctor recommended taking up gentle exercise because he was working too hard. When a friend visited from America, he challenged him to a game, and today's competition developed from that.

St Albans is also famed for its food and drink. The abbey is where hot cross buns originated. And given that the city has more pubs per square mile than any other in England, it will come as no surprise to learn that the Campaign For Real Ale (CAMRA) began here, in 1974, in the Farriers pub on Lower Dagnall Street. The pub has a blue plaque celebrating the fact.

Ye Olde Fighting Cocks is another old pub, reputed to be the oldest in England and recorded as such in the

Guinness Book of Records. This pub makes an ideal starting point to explore the Roman origins of Verulamium before making your way up the hill to the cathedral. In the winter, there is always a welcoming open fire, and in the summer the beer garden is a great place to relax. The strange name and layout of the pub stems from this being a cock pit at one time. The well of the pub was where the fights took place. The cellars are said to contain tunnels that lead to the abbey, which were used by the monks. As the home of CAMRA, you should try the real ales, particularly if McMullen's is on tap – this beer has been brewed in Hertfordshire for nearly 200 years.

St Albans, then, is a city full of firsts and superlatives – the first Christian martyr, the only English pope, the finest mosaics, the longest nave and the oldest pub, to name but a few.

THE COTSWOLDS – A DAY TOUR, AND MORE

JOHN BLAKEY

'Quintessential' is perhaps the word most associated with the Cotswolds. 'The Cotswolds are quintessentially English,' people say. I can't argue with that. A quintessence is the perfect embodiment of something, and the Cotswolds are what visitors from overseas, and we, the English, believe England *ought* to look like.

The Cotswolds have everything an ardent Anglophile could want – achingly beautiful ancient towns, sleepy villages, quirky country mansions, imposing castles and little stone cottages with doorways so low that most people must stoop to go through them. And all this is set among rolling green hills and magical forests as beautiful today as they ever were. This is no accident. The Cotswolds are highly protected by law as an area of outstanding natural beauty. Then, to top it off, throw in scones and jam, clotted cream, Earl Grey tea and last – most importantly – sheep.

Sheep? What, you may ask, have sheep to do with anything? Everything is the answer. The exact meaning of the word 'Cotswolds' (as also discussed on p 46) goes back too far for there not to be controversy, but it is said that 'cots' means sheep pens and 'wolds' are upland rolling hills. So the name means 'sheep pens in rolling hills'. The historic importance of these sheep, their pens and the rolling hills they graze cannot be overstated. It was probably the Romans who introduced sheep with very long wool, crossed them with local breeds and eventually produced a big, heavy-boned, long-maned breed known as the Cotswold Lion, which became the star performer in the lucrative world of wool. There was a saying in the twelfth century that 'in Europe, the best wool is English, and in England the best wool is Cotswold'. English wool merchants encouraged that reputation by exporting across the known world. The idyllic Cotswold countryside we see today was the economic powerhouse of England until the Industrial Revolution.

Wool brought unimaginable wealth to the merchant class, giving them the wherewithal not only to educate their children, but importantly, to build with stone. These newly rich merchants built many of the cottages, houses and inns we see today. Stone was expensive, and elsewhere, towns of similar age comprised wooden buildings with thatched roofs, which have long since rotted or burned down.

For the purposes of this tour of the Cotswolds, the following is a vaguely circular driving route, which you can join at any point. Some places are recommended for further exploration on foot, and there are numerous options for accommodation. The Cotswolds is a huge area, and while it isn't possible to take in all of its beautiful towns and villages, the route has been chosen to show off its variety. As for how long the route will take – that's up to you. Most of it can be covered in a single full day, if you can resist the temptation to stop everywhere! Otherwise, consider finding a room in a lovely old inn and spending two days and a night. Sites marked ** are separate excursions and will take one to two hours each. I recommend choosing to visit one or two of these places if you have only one day, and do check opening times in advance.

We'll begin at Woodstock, just north of Oxford on the A44 and the first of the Cotswolds' towns as you come from the south-east. Turning off the main road into High Street, you are immediately struck by the sheer amount of lovely honey-coloured limestone. We will see this stone throughout our journey; it gives the area its famous warm, welcoming glow.

The majority of roofs you see are made with stone tiles. Each roof bears hundreds of slices of stone about 25mm (an inch) thick. It is a miracle of old engineering that these roofs have not collapsed under their own weight, although many have buckled and bowed.

Woodstock's streets are unusually wide, as they are in a number of Cotswold towns, and the reason is – you guessed it – sheep. Walk along High Street and into Park

Street and you'll be following in the cloven hoofprints of hundreds of thousands of them. This town was built for the express purpose of buying and selling sheep, and the wide streets were designed to accommodate large flocks for both inspection and auction.

Do take note of the creeper-clad Bear Hotel, a creaking former coaching inn. Wander in; maybe have a drink. Richard Burton and Elizabeth Taylor loved to escape from the world here, staying in the Marlborough Suite, which comes complete with carved four-poster bed.

We will see many coaching inns on our travels. When the wool industry began in the 1200s, the wool traders needed somewhere to lay their heads and be fed, as did their horses and grooms. The stables were usually through the large arched entrances with the groom's quarters above the stalls.

Across the street from the Bear Hotel are the stocks. This is where wrongdoers would be secured by the legs. Passers-by were encouraged to throw rotten fruit, fish, eggs and offal at the offenders – punishment by humiliation. Unusually, though, as you'll see, this town provided its criminals with a roof over their heads in case of rain!

At the end of Park Street, you'll find Chaucer's House, where some say the author of the *Canterbury Tales* once had a property. Just around the corner is an entrance to **Blenheim Palace, birthplace of Sir Winston Churchill. He is buried on the other side of the estate, in St Martin's churchyard, Bladon.

As reward for winning the Battle of Blenheim in 1704, Queen Anne gave Sir Winston's ancestor, Sir John Churchill, the Duke of Marlborough, the manor of Woodstock and a vast fortune to build a palace. The estate was passed down through the family, but money dwindled, since aristocrats could not be seen to work, and by the time the 9th Duke inherited in 1892, bankruptcy loomed. He had two choices – sell, or marry money. The American railroad heiress Consuelo Vanderbilt was forced by her title-hungry mother to marry the Duke in 1895 and her dowry secured the Churchill family home. The family still live in this amazing palace, surrounded by grounds designed by the aptly named Lancelot 'Capability' Brown, who aimed to create gardens that looked as though nature herself had designed them – but better.

Leaving Woodstock, continue up the A44, through Chipping Norton, one of the bigger Cotswold towns. Three miles the other side of Chipping Norton, turn left on the A436 to **Chastleton House, following signs to the house along winding lanes for 1½ miles. From the car park, take the lovely walk down through the field to the house. This dusty, cobweb-covered, unrestored Jacobean manor house was built in the early 1600s by a wool merchant keen to make a statement about his wealth and power.

Returning to the A436, turn right, drive two miles, then turn left to the Oddingtons. Here you will find not only two lovely villages, but two inns renowned for their food – the Fox in Lower Oddington and the Horse and Groom in Upper Oddington. Both are atmospheric stone-flagged inns from the 1500s with charming accommodation. Between the villages, look out for the lane to the eleventh-century bijou church of St Nicholas – a gem complete with doom paintings to alert a largely illiterate medieval congregation to the dangers of bad behaviour.

Follow signs for Stow-on-the-Wold. Stow means 'holy place' and 'wold' means rolling hills. You'll see on the map that eight roads radiate from Stow, like a spider's legs. All roads lead to Stow ... indicating just how important this town once was. The disproportionate number of inns and hotels in the town, built to accommodate the travelling wool traders, convey the same message. Find a parking space and take twenty minutes to wander, noticing the unusual piazza-like town square. One theory is that the square was built like this to protect the market traders from the wind, since the town is in a particularly high and exposed position. The stone market cross looms up on one side of the square to remind traders to be fair in their dealings – God is watching. At the same end of the square, note the extremely narrow alleys between buildings. These are called 'tures' and were built this way to allow sheep through into the market square one at a time, so that they could be counted and inspected.

The Norman church here, St Edward's, was used in 1646 to imprison a thousand Royalist soldiers after the final battle of the English Civil War at nearby Donnington. In Digbeth Street, The Royalist Hotel is reportedly the oldest inn in England. Travellers have rested here since the year 947.

Taking the A429, we're now off towards Moreton-in-Marsh. Built on the Fosse Way (the Roman road from Exeter to Lincoln via Bath) and linked to London and the Midlands by rail, Moreton hosts the largest modern-day market in the Cotswolds. Every Tuesday, its streets are filled with stalls full of fruit, vegetables, crafts and curiosities.

Rejoin the A44 towards Evesham. For those with time, 1⅓ miles outside Moreton, Batsford has an arboretum as well as the delightful **Cotswold Falconry Centre where, in ancient meadows surrounded by forest, you can get close to eagles, owls and hawks and, at certain times, see them put through their paces in entertaining and educational aerial displays. Book ahead for the opportunity to handle and work with the birds yourself. Opposite the entrance to the centre is **Sezincote, an extraordinary house built in the Mogul style of Rajasthan – complete with waterfalls, grottos and minarets. Visited at various times by Sir John Betjeman and the future George IV, it inspired the poem 'Summoned by Bells' by the first and the building of Brighton Pavilion by the second.

Our tour now takes us between the cascades of cottages in Bourton-on-the-Hill and continues for four miles to a right turn to Chipping Campden. As you descend the hill, you'll see the village nestling in the valley. The flat-topped hill beyond the town is Dover's Hill, a natural amphitheatre where the 'Cotswold Olympicks' are held. Founded by local lawyer Robert Dover in 1612 and now held on spring bank holidays, events include tug-of-war, shin kicking, piano smashing, judo and dwile flonking, in which teams fling (or flonk) an ale soaked cloth (or dwile) at each other as they dance. The referee (or jobanowl) awards points according to which body parts are hit! It's been suggested that Dover was trying to break down class distinctions with his Olympicks, as rich and poor alike took part.

A word about the drystone walls in this area. It's a real art to build and maintain them but they have an advantage over walls using mortar. Stone and mortar heat up and cool down at different rates, so a wall built using mortar will eventually 'blow' and fall apart. On the other hand, a drystone wall, built without mortar, when well made, should not collapse unless pushed. Along with hedgerows, these form the 'cots', or sheep pens, of the Cotswolds.

On the left-hand side as you enter Chipping Campden are some of the finest thatched houses anywhere. Cotswold thatch is usually made from wheat straw tightly bound to create a waterproof, highly insulating layer overhead. Well made, a good thatch can last about thirty years. Before ceilings became common in houses, rooms used to be open to the roof, and insects living in the thatch would drop on unsuspecting sleepers, bringing about the introduction of canopied beds. These beds had horsehair mattresses supported by ropes, which need tightening regularly; the combination of this and the protective canopy is said to have given rise to the expression, 'Sleep tight, don't let the bed bugs bite.'

Chipping means 'market', so you can perhaps guess, as you go down Sheep Street towards the village centre, what this town's main industry was. Many believe that this is the loveliest village in the Cotswolds; it's certainly a contender. The sweep of terraced cottages is a delight. Pass the covered market built in 1627 and almost opposite Church Street is Grevel House, which has a gated archway and mullioned windows. This is the oldest and perhaps finest in this street of fine houses. William Grevel, an extremely wealthy wool merchant, is thought to be the inspiration for the merchant in Chaucer's *Canterbury Tales*, and it was his money that was largely responsible for the building of the impressive church of St James in Church Street.

Straight on from Grevel House, a lovely fifteen-minute signposted drive will bring you to two beautiful gardens, both open to the public. **Hidcote is a wonderful series of 'outdoor rooms' created by American Lawrence Johnston. Johnston studied at Cambridge and, after graduating, fought with the British army in the First World War. He was so badly injured that he was laid out for burial, but thankfully someone noticed him move slightly. His mother Gertrude bought Hidcote and Lawrence took to gardening. Each 'room' has a different character from the next, and the overall effect is enchanting. Just a short distance away, and built on a vertiginous slope, is **Kiftsgate. The more intimate domestic gardens here are certainly worth a wander. If you have been to look at either or both gardens, retrace your steps to Chipping Campden to continue.

From Chipping Campden, go back up to the A44, turn right and drive just over three miles to Broadway. Do take in the whole length of the village, because each end is quite different in character. The quieter end has some exquisitely beautiful houses and is more uniformly elegant than Chipping Campden. Note the ornamental mushroom-shaped stones in front of some houses. These are called staddle stones, and barns, granaries and game larders were once built upon them to protect their contents from vermin and damp.

Another ancient coaching inn is the Lygon Arms. There is not a straight line in the entire building, as though the whole place has sagged beneath the weight of time. Both leaders of the Civil War stayed here, Charles I in 1645 and Oliver Cromwell in 1651. It has low doors, beamed ceilings and, in winter, huge open fires. For those considering a special overnight stay, the Lygon Arms is an option, as is nearby Buckland Manor Hotel. This has the feel of a grand private country mansion. Dating from the 1200s, it is set in beautiful grounds and has its own church.

Taking the road to the right of the Broadway Hotel, follow signs for Snowshill. Pronounced locally as Snozzle, this remote little village is built around a triangular green. **Snowshill Manor is open to the public. Charles Wade, an archetypal English eccentric, collected anything and everything he felt was exquisitely made and restored the house to display it. He packed the manor with everything from clocks and cowbells to suits of samurai armour. Appropriately, the family motto was 'Let Nothing Perish'.

From Snowshill village, follow signs to Snowshill Lavender, where, in summer, the fields are ablaze with blue. On a sunny day, nothing can compare with the sight and scent of these lavender fields. At the top of the hill, turn right towards Stow. Here you realise that half the joy of the Cotswolds is the journey between destinations.

Well before Stow itself, turn left to Upper Swell and after five miles turn right for Lower Swell. Why the name Swell? It comes from well, as in water. In 1807 a spring containing iron salts was discovered here and, taking advantage of the fashion for spas, locals tried in vain to encourage people to come here to 'take the waters', as they did in Bath.

Now follow the signs for the Slaughters, turning right for Upper Slaughter by the gates of a house named

Copse Hill. People presume that something awful must have happened in the Slaughters, but 'slohtre' is simply an ancient word for 'muddy place'. The Slaughters, Upper and Lower, are places to switch off the car engine and listen to the silence. Continuing to Lower Slaughter, don't miss the grand gates to Upper Slaughter Manor. The gravel drive is straight out of a Jane Austen novel, only needing Mr Darcy to come striding out in his breeches. This house in this setting is, I think, the most beautiful in all the Cotswolds. Lower Slaughter's idle stream, the River Eye, is spanned by a number of ancient stone footbridges. On the other side of the river is a corn mill from the 1880s.

Leave the village, passing Lower Slaughter Manor Hotel on your left. At the A429, turn left towards Stow. Pass Fosse Manor Hotel on the left, then turn right on to the A424 to Burford. Burford was recently voted one of *Forbes* magazine's top ten places to live in the world, and as you cross the 700-year-old bridge across the River Windrush and into High Street, it's easy to see why. Take the second left into Church Lane and follow signs to the car park. Now walk back to St John the Baptist church, parts of which are around 900 years old. This huge church, like many others in the Cotswolds, built with the immense profits of the wool trade, and many of the tombs in the graveyard are shaped like woolsacks.

On the outside of the church, to the left of the door, you'll see the names of three soldiers, leaders of a movement called the Levellers, which was formed during the Civil War. The Levellers were radicals, who supported religious toleration and equality for all before the law. Opposed to Charles I and his autocratic ways, they supported Oliver Cromwell and fought, literally, for the removal of political, social and economic inequalities – the 'levelling' of society. However, after the king had been executed and an English republican commonwealth created, Cromwell took the role of Lord Protector, and the Levellers came to believe that he was ruling in a dictatorial way. So they started to fight against him, and these three were captured and executed on Cromwell's orders.

Walk to High Street and turn left up the hill. From here can be seen the fine array of shops and inns lining the street in the foreground, and beautiful cottages tumbling down the hill behind. Although this town was built on the back of the wool industry, other important industries developed later, such as the local quarries. Not only is stone from here found all over the Cotswolds, but it was also used to build Blenheim Palace, St Paul's

Cathedral in London and many of the Oxford colleges.

With better roads in the 1700s came the golden era of coaching and Burford grew to be an important stop along the Cheltenham–Oxford–London route, becoming unusually cosmopolitan as a result. The introduction of the railways killed the coaching industry in the mid-1800s. Trains shrank Britain to one-fifth of its previous size timewise and meant, among other things, that even in the middle of England, people could get fresh fish from the coast for the first time. It seems fitting to end our tour of this beautiful part of England at the ancient and award-winning Lamb Inn – and, of course, it is in Sheep Street.

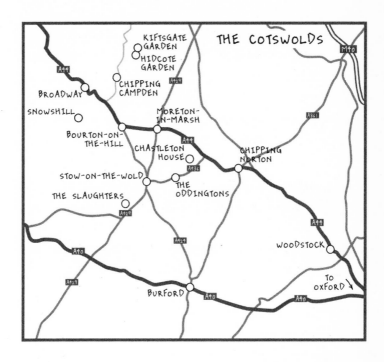

SALISBURY AND STONEHENGE – FAITH AND MYSTERY

RICHARD BARTLETT

When you arrive in Salisbury by train, rather than follow the crowds into the city centre, turn right as you leave the station car park and walk down to the river. From here, if you stand on 'the town path', which runs through the water meadows, you will see a view that has not changed for hundreds of years. This is where John Constable, one of the great English painters of the nineteenth century, sketched his iconic view of Salisbury Cathedral – its majestic presence towering over the trees and ancient buildings of the close, set to perfection by the river and the meadows in the foreground. The cathedral's foundation stones were laid in 1220 and the beautiful building was consecrated just thirty-eight years later. However, the tower and spire were not added until the early 1300s. The spire is still the loftiest in England at 124 metres (406 feet) high.

The first great church in these parts was built at Sarum during the reign of William I, or William the Conqueror as he is more usually known. William realised that the best way to rule his new kingdom was to have power bases dotted around the country, and at Sarum, which had been a Roman fort, he built a great keep and barracks for his soldiers. His nephew, Osmond, a leading figure of the Catholic church, wanted to build a cathedral there and with permission from the pope and the king, building began. To have two powerful institutions – the church and the state – operating in such close proximity was never going to be easy and soon a new church was begun in Salisbury, two miles to the south. Bishop Richard Poore, now in charge, had decided that for the good of the church it should leave Sarum's inhospitable natural environment and military presence and move south.

Although the land around Salisbury is largely water meadow and liable to flooding, the cathedral was built, with shallow foundations, on a shelf of granite chippings. Bishop Poore gave 27.5 hectares (68 acres) of land for the church, which was to be surrounded by a graveyard. Clerics were encouraged to build their houses encircling this, in a formation known as a close. By this time, the town of Sarum had been more or less abandoned, and the stone from the cathedral there was brought to Salisbury and used to build a defensive wall around the new cathedral and close. This is how it remains today, and the town gate of the close is still locked at 10.30 every night.

Keeping the river to your right, walk towards the cathedral. You will soon come to the crane bridge, and looking to the other side of the river you will see an imposing house. This was originally a wool merchant's house of the 1400s. Salisbury's wealth came from sheep and at this time Salisbury was the tenth wealthiest city in England. Many of the merchants showed off their wealth by building large houses. In the 1500s, the house here was acquired by Lord Audley, who made alterations to it, but didn't get to enjoy the building for too long. Some time later, he was thrown in the Tower of London and beheaded for 'depraved bestiality'. The town took over the building and it was used as a workhouse for the poor before being bought by the diocese of Salisbury for its headquarters.

Now cross the ancient stone bridge. Anthony Trollope, one of the great literary talents of the nineteenth century, would have crossed this same bridge; his inspiration for the *Barchester Chronicles* was taken from the buildings and people of Salisbury. Turn left after crossing the bridge and walk along, keeping the river to your left. Crossing over Bridge Street, in front of you is an old mill, until recently known as Bishop's Mill, because it was owned by the church. Five rivers ran through the town, and woollen mills were built on their banks to harness the water's power to drive the water wheels that powered the looms that wove the wool into cloth. In the case of Bishop's Mill, the river was diverted to run under the mill and the race is still to be seen as we cross the little bridge by its side.

We now come to the church of St Thomas and St Edmund, built as a place of worship for the workers and craftsmen who were building the cathedral. Originally a humble wooden church, it was rebuilt in stone in the 1400s. Inside, there is an extraordinary doom painting over the chancel arch. In those days, all churches were Catholic and it was taught that when you died you went to purgatory and from there, on the day of judgement, you would either rise up into heaven or sink into hell. This is what a doom painting showed in all its glory. After the Reformation of the sixteenth century, these paintings were often covered with whitewash. The doom painting here was discovered under its layer of whitewash in the 1800s.

Keeping the church to your right and walking around the graveyard, you will come out on the edge of the market square. A charter from Henry III in the 1100s gave permission for the establishment of a market in the town, and a market still thrives here today. As you walk through the square, where stallholders still cry out their wares, notice the street names – Fish Row, Oatmeal Row and Butchers Row. If you leave the square by the exit on your right, you will come to the poultry cross. The hexagonal shaft that holds up the stone canopy and cross was erected in the 1400s. On market days, poultry was displayed and sold here, sheltered from inclement weather. The cross overhead reassured customers that they would get a fair trade. Surrounding the market place, a number of half-timbered houses have survived, today used as either shops or pubs.

The high street of Salisbury leads up to the gates of the close and the cathedral beyond. Situated here – on your left – is The George, one of the half-timbered coaching inns built in the sixteenth century. Before the railways arrived in the middle of the nineteenth century, you would have arrived in Salisbury by horse-drawn coach, which would have deposited you in the yard of a coaching inn. Sadly, today the yard of The George is the site of a shopping mall.

There is now just one street to cross before entering the gates of the close. Look to the left as you do so and you will see The New Inn, a rather fine half-timbered hostelry that was 'new' in the 1400s. Above the gates in front of you is the coat of arms for Charles II, placed here at the end of the 1600s to commemorate the restoration of the monarchy after the Civil War.

You have now arrived in the celebrated close. Here you step back in time, away from the hustle and bustle of the city's busy streets, to a place that is both quiet and restful. The houses you see were built between the thirteenth and nineteenth centuries. Some are still owned by the church, the larger ones have been put to use as museums or schools, but the majority of the houses are privately owned. All sit harmoniously together, their gardens flower-filled in summer, surrounding the cathedral. One of the first buildings you observe on the left-hand side is the long, low, red-bricked 'college of matrons', a fine house of the mid-seventeenth century with a white cupola atop. It was built by Seth Ward who, when a teenager, had fallen in love with a young girl of the town. However, her affections went to a clergyman, whom she married, and the couple left Salisbury for Exeter, many miles away. Wade remained a bachelor and by the time he was sixty years old had become a bishop. He then discovered that the girl he knew had fallen on hard times and was now a widow, still living in Exeter. He decided to help her, in a very discreet way, by building this house for church widows of the Diocese of Salisbury ... and Exeter.

Now bear right, crossing diagonally over Choristers Green. A cathedral will always have a professional choir of men and boys, the men being paid, and the boys educated, by the church. In front of you is the Wren Hall that was the choir school in the seventeenth century and is now used for other educational pursuits. On the right-hand side of the green is Mompesson House, an eighteenth-century gem, now in the guardianship of the National Trust and well worth a visit. In the far corner of the green stands one of the older buildings, the Bishop's Wardrobe. This was once the bishop's lodging and storeroom but also where the clerics' fine vestments were kept. Today it is a military museum.

You now pass another charming double-fronted house, set well back behind wrought-iron gates, which was once owned and lived in by a former prime minister, Sir Edward Heath. He is commemorated with a tombstone set in the floor in the crossing of the cathedral. Past this you will come to the King's House, named after James I, who resided here at times during his reign in the 1600s. The house dates from the 1400s, with later additions and alterations apparent from the front façade. The original house was constructed using local flint and stone but for its refurbishment and extension in later centuries brick was used.

During the nineteenth and early twentieth centuries, the King's House was a college for the training of female teachers, the College of Sarum St Michael. Author Thomas Hardy's two sisters attended the college, and one day, while waiting for them, Hardy wandered into the cathedral and there started a conversation with a stone mason, who was working on one of the tombs. From this meeting he was inspired to write his last major novel, *Jude the Obscure*, the story of a stone mason working in a cathedral, who falls in love with a young girl training in a teachers' training college.

Now that much of the cathedral has been restored and cleaned, you can really appreciate what pilgrims would have seen on their arrival at the church's glorious west front. The life-sized statues on five levels under the mighty Christ in Majesty at the apex are a testament to the faith of the countless people who have worked on, or been part of, this great cathedral. Originally, the statues would have been even more splendid since they were painted and gilded; sadly, today only faint traces of colour remain, in the figures above the great west door.

Look to the first level of statues from the ground on the left-hand side – not the man on the corner but the one next to him. He wears a pointed hat, which is a bishop's mitre, and has a swathing cloak. Look carefully at what he holds in his hand and you will see that it is a model of the original church, for this is Bishop Richard Poore. Notice that the model comes without the tower and steeple, which were added in the early fourteenth century.

Now enter the cathedral and look down the nave. Note its soaring height. This is a beautiful example of early English Gothic architecture. You are looking east towards the high altar. All churches are built east to west, and the east end is where building would have begun in 1220. Looking around, almost all you see was built within the next thirty-eight years, and because of the speed of its construction, there is a unity in the architecture rarely seen in England. The stone is from a nearby quarry in Chilmark. The thin pillars, placed down the nave and crossing, are of Purbeck marble, from Dorset, and it is these that really hold up the weight of the roof. When this church was built, we were a Catholic nation, so try to imagine the scene with small chapels down either side of the nave dedicated to various saints and martyrs. There would have been no seating in the nave, just a number of stone tombs. This area would have been used for processions. The flickering of candles, the smell of incense and perhaps the singing and chanting of the priests behind the choir screen would have stirred a sense of wonder and awe in the pilgrims. By all accounts, the entire church would have been highly decorated in very bright colours.

Walk down the nave and there on your left you will see the oldest working mechanical clock in England, made in 1386 – hard to tell the time by this clock since it was made without a face. You just listened for the clock to strike the hour. In front of you is the surprising new font, crucifix in shape, with a span of three metres (ten feet) to allow full-immersion baptism. Move on to the crossing of the church and look up. Way above your head there is what seems a fairly small hole in the ceiling but it is actually over two metres (six feet) in diameter. Above this is the windlass – an old wooden pulley that was used during the building of the tower and steeple to bring stone blocks up from the ground. Look down and you will see a plaque indicating that, due to settlement, the steeple is now a metre (just over three feet) off true – not surprising when you consider it weighs over 6,000 tonnes.

The cathedral's choir stalls are the largest and oldest complete set in the country. They were made in 1236 from oak provided by Henry III. If you can, look under one of the choir stall seats to see the delightful carving of the misericords. On your right is the wonderfully carved seat or throne of the bishop. This, in Latin, is a *'cathedra'*, and hence 'cathedral'. Finally, look towards the east window. Obviously modern, this was installed in the 1980s. It looks, from a distance, as if it is made up of random pieces of glass, but if you look closer, you will see faces in the window. It is dedicated to prisoners of conscience, those who have been imprisoned or died for their beliefs. Note that it is for *their* beliefs and not necessarily those of this church. Such thinking would not, one imagines, have been tolerated when this ancient church was built.

If you leave the church by the south transept door, you will be in the largest cloisters in England, and from here you can enter the Chapter House, which was built in the latter part of the thirteenth century. It is an extraordinary room with a fan vault that rises from a central pillar. Around the walls, a beautiful stone frieze depicts Old Testament stories. The document displayed in the glass case warrants serious attention – one of only four original copies of the Magna Carta and the best preserved of them all.

Leaving Salisbury, if you are travelling to Stonehenge, avoid the busy main roads and instead take the road that meanders through the Woodford valley. On your way, you will pass the site of Sarum, thatched cottages, Norman churches, old working farms and even a couple of rather grand stone manor houses. Soon, in the distance, on sloping ground you will find Stonehenge.

As you walk towards the monument, hold back a little so you can take it all in. On the ground in front of you there is a ditch that encircles the stones; the soil from this has been made into a bank just on the inside of the ditch. This ditch and bank is the 'henge'. Stones stand within, so 'Stonehenge'. Around 3000 BC, before the stone was brought here, some form of timber construction was encircled by the ditch and bank, a woodhenge, and from this time onwards it would have been a place of worship.

By 2500 BC, stones had been brought into the circle. The two smaller upright stones, almost in the middle of the circle, were among the first. These are examples of the bluestones that came from the Preseli Mountains, in Wales, about 240 miles away. They were erected in a kind of double semi-circle, but before the circle was complete, the larger sarsen stones, from the Marlborough Downs about 20 miles away, were introduced. These were erected as a circle of upright stones with stone lintels above.

The largest of the stones were kept for the middle of the circle and these were used to make five trilithons – each one comprising a pair of upright stones linked by a lintel. These were placed in a horseshoe shape with the opening facing the Heel Stone, which you will see just outside the henge to the north-east. A large stone placed at the centre of the horseshoe is known as the Altar Stone. Over the next thousand years, Stonehenge's builders kept realigning the bluestones until they had formed most of them into a circle within the sarsen circle and the others into a horseshoe within the trilithons.

Now approach the stones. Stonehenge is unique because all the stones have been dressed by hammering shallow grooves to remove the rough surface, and the uprights have been made to taper in towards the top. Holes had to be dug in the ground in which to place the uprights to ensure they did not fall over. Stone hammers were used on the stone while deer antlers and the bones of cattle were used in the making of the holes. The tops of the upright stones all had to be the same distance up from the ground so that the lintels would sit level, but the stones are of different heights. Therefore the depth of the holes was crucial. To make sure the lintels could not fall off, mortise and tenon joints were worked in the stone of the lintels and uprights. The lintels of the outer circle are also locked, end-to-end, by vertical tongue and groove joints. Considering the weight and size of the stones, Stonehenge is perhaps one of the greatest achievements of prehistoric man in Europe.

Now walk about a quarter of the circle, making sure that you can see the Heel Stone on the far side. This stone was placed so that the sun would rise behind it on the summer solstice (the longest day of the year) and its first rays flood into the heart of Stonehenge. In the seventeenth

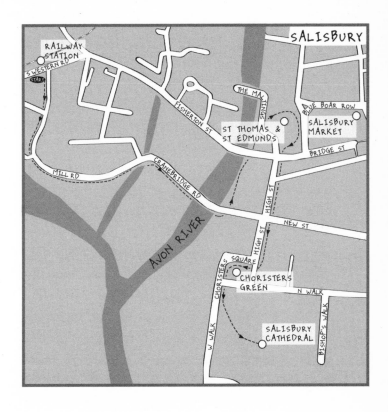

century, two amateur archaeologists and antiquaries visited here, John Aubrey and William Stukeley. Aubrey was the first person to make an accurate drawing of the site, recording as he did so a series of indentations in the ground just within the bank. Excavations 250 years later showed that these indentations were the remains of a series of 56 holes in which timber uprights had been placed. They are now known as the Aubrey Holes.

Stukeley for his part concluded that it was Druid priests who had built Stonehenge, an incorrect deduction but for centuries this was what was believed about the origin of the circle and its stones.

Walk another quarter of the circle and now you should be able to see a grass-covered mound in the field behind you. This is a Beaker burial site, known as a barrow. It was the Beakers, in fact, who built Stonehenge. On their great feast days, they would have processed along the avenue that led them past the Heel Stone into the great circle, chanting and carrying flaming torches.

Today, at the summer solstice, people from all walks of life stay here overnight, singing and carrying their own torches to watch the sun rise, as folk have done for many thousands of years. This extraordinary site, bathed in mystery, is a wonder of ancient achievement that continues to hold visitors enthralled.

BLETCHLEY PARK – TOP SECRET

REX OSBORN

There are historic battlefields, Gettysburg in the United States, Waterloo in Belgium and many more, where visitors follow maps of a conflict and, with eyes closed, imagine the sounds of swordstroke and gunfire and the cries of the dying, and it is possible to stand on the very spot where many fell. When we stroll past the unprepossessing blockhouses at the entrance to Bletchley Park, we step on to an historic battlefield where there was no swordplay or gunfire and there are no tragic lines of the fallen. However, this was the site of a gruelling action as decisive as any in war. The intelligence victory won at Bletchley Park made victory possible in numerous battles around the world, shortened the Second World War and saved thousands of lives. And success came thanks to an invention that, these days, many of us use at our desks every day and even carry in our pockets – the computer.

A tour of Bletchley Park, north-west of London, starts at Block B, where visitors buy their admission tickets and are given information on how to plan their visit. While most of Bletchley Park was devoted to German codes, it was in Block B that Italian Air, Italian Naval and much of the Japanese code-breaking was located in the Second World War. Here is the main exhibition that explains the decoding work of wartime Bletchley Park. A poignant display shows two mannequins in authentic period uniforms, German soldiers from a signal unit (the 65th Nachrichten Abteilung), one of whom strikes a determined pose, standing among his Enigma cypher equipment. He peers thoughtfully ahead of him as though confident that he and the German forces are strong, well equipped and will be victorious. What he does not know is that every message he sends or receives is being intercepted by the British, together with all Enigma traffic and numerous other types of coded signals.

At Bletchley Park during the war, enemy signals were deciphered, translated and analysed in order that Allied forces in the field could always be a step ahead of the Axis powers. How it was done, how important it was, and its impact on our lives today is the story told here at the Bletchley Park National Codes Centre.

The Enigma machine was a kind of specialised portable typewriter that scrambled messages using a group of rotors slotted in the top. Several such machines are on display in Block B. The first Enigma devices had been made in Germany in peacetime so that banks could exchange financially sensitive information. The machines were available commercially in the inter-war years, but when the German armed forces realised the potential of these devices, they took over production. Messages scrambled into code by one Enigma machine at one German military post could be radioed to another post and remain unreadable until retyped into an Enigma machine there, the rotors of which had been turned to the same position as those of the sender's machine. Of all the enemy codes handled by cryptanalysts at Bletchley Park, the Enigma cipher system and its more advanced successor, based on the Lorenz machine, were the hardest and the most important to break.

Bletchley Park was the home of London financier and Liberal politician Sir Herbert Samuel Leon – Sammy to his friends. He lived there with his wife, Lady Fanny Leon, and their family from 1883. Sir Herbert died in 1926 and Lady Fanny in 1937. At the heart of their estate was a grand farmhouse, which they steadily enlarged. Sir Herbert's initials, HLS, fixed in large letters over the door, which now forms the main entrance to the mansion, were not the most ostentatious feature of the house. Sir Herbert had exotic tastes in architecture and they changed often. That same door is guarded by two large griffins, placed there during Sir Herbert's flamboyant Victorian Gothic phase. At other times he favoured Tudor Baroque and Dutch Baroque styles. The result is a teeming conglomeration of eccentrically assembled styles that bemused, and in some cases horrified, the code-breakers based at Bletchley Park. Renowned historian Peter Calvocoressi recorded his memories of serving at the code base in his book *Top Secret Ultra*, published in 1980, and says of the house: 'Even from the more generous or quizzical standpoint of today it is not a striking example of the taste of its times and inside it was dreadful.' Turning to the interiors he describes 'a lot of heavy wooden panelling enlivened here and there by Alhambresque (Leicester Square, not Granada, Andalusia) decorative fancies'. Yale history professor Robin Winks, in his book *Cloak and Gown: Scholars in America's Secret War* (1987), quotes architect Landis Gores, an American code-breaker at Bletchley. His comments on the house are harsher than Calvocoressi's: 'a maudlin and monstrous pile probably unsurpassed, though not for lack of competition, in the

architectural gaucherie of the mid-Victorian era ...
hopelessly vulgarised by extensive porches and solaria as
well as by batteries of tall casements in intermittent
profusion ... altogether inchoate, unfocused and
incomprehensible, not to say indigestible.'

Even film makers have not warmed to the mansion.
When *Enigma* came to be filmed in 2001, Chicheley
Hall stood in for Bletchley Park. Chicheley Hall was the
country house where Special Operations Executive
agents trained during the Second World War.

British wartime planners feared London would be
devastated by aerial bombardment in the event of war,
so it was decided that a rural base would be best for the
code-breakers, and the mansion and grounds of
Bletchley Park provided some essential features.

The network of vital communication lines that ran
around Bletchley Park could hardly have been better
configured. The A5 trunk road ran past the estate,
stretching from London across the Midlands to
Holyhead, and the General Post Office had laid a major
telephone trunk line along the route. Two important rail
lines ran through Bletchley railway station, close by –
one to London and, significantly, one between Oxford
and Cambridge with Bletchley conveniently at about the
midpoint between these two university towns. If you visit

Bletchley Park by rail, you will get a sense of what a close, interlocking fit this combination was as you cross the road from the station to the park. Also nearby was the teleprinter network repeater station at Fenny Stratford.

Bletchley Park had its own code name – Station X. From August 1939 a mock medieval tower in the centre of the mansion contained a radio room for contact with British embassies in Europe. As Bletchley Park was the tenth in a group of intelligence bases, the radio station was given the Roman numeral X. The radio was moved out for security reasons in January 1940 but the name Station X stuck as the code name for the Bletchley Park site.

Initially, the estate's buildings were considered sufficient for the projected force of code-breakers but as the site's function grew ever more essential to the war effort, so the force and its infrastructure grew in size. A year before the outbreak of the Second World War, the Government Code and Cypher School were already staffing the rooms of the mansion. Appropriately, the school's advance team arrived disguised as Captain Ridley's Shooting Party. By war's end, roughly 10,000 staff, some 6,000 of them women, all billeted in nearby towns, worked at Bletchley Park in three shifts that ran round the clock – 8 a.m. till 4 p.m.; 4 p.m. till midnight;

midnight till 8 a.m. From early 1939, extra work space had to be created and the somewhat makeshift timber huts and concrete-frame blocks were added, as need arose. Today, stark and spartan, they cluster incongruously around the red-brick mansion, housing various museums and exhibits.

The first of the code-breakers to be brought in at the start of the war were those who had worked in Room 40, a legendary code-breaking section that operated during the First World War, including Dillwyn (Dilly) Knox. Then came mathematicians, such as Alan Turing, linguists and classicists, especially those who had experience of reading hieroglyphics and ancient dead languages, and a variety of other specialists who were deemed academic and trustworthy enough to work on code-breaking. According to one story, at the beginning of 1942, under the cover of an argument in the *Daily Telegraph* letters column about how fast that paper's crossword could be completed, a competition was held in the *Telegraph* newsroom in Fleet Street in London. Twenty or so competitors turned up to see who could do the crossword fastest. They all finished it within thirteen minutes and the winner got a cigarette lighter as a prize. Soon afterwards, all the competitors were approached by the War Office to be trained as code-breakers.

A system for decrypting German Enigma messages by mechanical means was first devised by Polish intelligence in the 1930s. Called Bomba (from *bomba kryptologiczna*, which is Polish for 'cryptologic bomb'), it spawned the family of war-winning decoding devices. In the late 1930s, Polish intelligence shared their information and technology with both Britain and France. Using this crucial knowledge, two Bletchley Park mathematicians, Alan Turing and Gordon Welchman, commissioned a mechanism they called the Bombe in March 1940, and a more sophisticated version, the Spider Bombe, in August of that year. The Bombe was a large electrical machine of over a hundred spinning drums. It stood about 1.8 metres (6 feet) tall and 2 metres (7 feet) long and tested possible Enigma code combinations at high speed. Different German services used different versions of Enigma, and different Enigma codes, so there were times early in the war when it was impossible to read certain Enigma messages. The most serious gap came in 1942 when German Navy Enigma traffic was unreadable for many months until the necessary codebooks were taken from German submarine U-559. Nevertheless, the Bombe became the main way for the Allies to read Enigma messages for the rest of the war.

To show the machines' wiring set-ups, operatives of the Women's Royal Naval Service (the WRNS), who mostly had the task of working the Bombes, were given ever-changing diagrams nicknamed 'menus' – a term that stuck and is used in basic computer terminology today.

So important were the Bombe machines that they were dispersed to avoid the danger of a chance air raid destroying them all. The United States, supplied with plans by Bletchley Park, built their own versions of the Bombes and these machines shared the decoding workload worldwide. By 1944, more than 200 Bombes were in use. A re-created Bombe can be seen in Hut 11.

In June 1941, Germany began using a new machine for top-level military communications. The machine, called Lorenz, was more advanced than Enigma. By November 1942, Bletchley Park personnel were able to break Lorenz ciphers manually, but this was dangerously slow work and mathematician Max Newman suggested getting a machine to do it at high speed. In June 1943, in response to Newman's suggestion, a new machine, called Robinson, was created to tackle Lorenz messages, but proved unreliable. Taking theories developed by Alan Turing in 1937, Newman supervised senior Post Office engineer Tommy Flowers in the construction of something quite new, the ground-breaking 'universal computing machine', code-named Colossus. With the completion of Colossus at the end of 1943, Lorenz became accessible to the Allies and the computer age had begun.

In response to changes in the Lorenz machines, a more sophisticated computer – Colossus Mk II – was brought into operation on 1 June 1944, in time for the D-Day landings. A re-creation of Colossus is on show in Bletchley's H Block.

One of the most striking items at the Bletchley Park centre today is a life-sized statue of Alan Turing, in slate, by sculptor Stephen Kettle. Of all the cryptanalysts at Bletchley Park during the Second World War, Turing's is the name that stands out. His inspiration and influence reached across so many of the problems and their solutions that preoccupied the code-breakers' station. Already working part-time for the Government Code and Cypher School before the war, Turing turned up for duty at Bletchley Park the day after Britain declared war. His mathematical genius helped crack codes the conventional way but also put him at the forefront of the construction of machines to speed up the work. His pre-war theories laid the foundations for the construction of the first computers.

In recent years, many have been moved by the fact that the contribution Turing's genius made to the Allied war effort went unrecognised because so much of his war work was top secret. Many also have been saddened by the injustice of Turing's post-war conviction for alleged indecency and his suicide in 1954. A number of computer scientists, historians, LGBT (lesbian, gay, bisexual and transgender) activists and others have come together to put this right. One of those moved by Turing's story, American philanthropist Sydney E. Frank, commissioned the slate sculpture. As well, the Turing Centenary Advisory Committee (TCAC), with involvement by the Bletchley Park Trust, was formed to organise events for the Alan Turing Year 2012, marking the 100th anniversary of Turing's birth. A good way to remember, understand and recognise the work of the man, a victim of prejudice himself, without whom our history might have been very different, is to visit the place where he did so much to defend our freedoms – Bletchley Park.

In the Second World War there was no intelligence operation more secret than the work of the code-breakers. If at any time the German forces had suspected that their 'impregnable' encoding system was compromised, they would have abandoned it and all the precious intelligence deployed by the Allies would have dried up. The work of Bletchley Park was cloaked in secrecy so strict that nobody let on for thirty-five years, and even then the full truth (if it is the full truth) emerged only fitfully.

Recognition of the importance of the Bletchley Park site diminished to the extent that by 1991 plans were mooted to demolish it and build a housing development and supermarket. The Bletchley Archaeological and Historical Society (BAHS) held what was to be a last Bletchley Park on-site staff reunion and 400 veterans attended. Inspired by such support, the BAHS decided to run a campaign to say 'No' to the development and to save the site. The campaign was long, hard and nearly faltered but eventually it succeeded, so that today the Bletchley Park Trust operate the site and it is open to the public.

To maintain such a large site, the Trust has had to follow a strategy of diversification, resulting in a number of varied but complementary museums and exhibitions being located at Bletchley Park. These include the National Museum of Computing; a display commemorating the Oxfordshire and Buckinghamshire Light Infantry, a local regiment, in its capture of Pegasus Bridge in Normandy on D-Day, 6 June 1944; the Pigeons at War display (the loft for the pigeons that were an important part of communications at wartime Bletchley Park can still be seen on your tour); and an astonishing collection of Churchill memorabilia.

Throughout this complex site, the Trust has taken great care over who and what it invites us to remember. The senior code-breakers are named, usually in association with their greatest breakthrough or at the cottage or hut where they worked. A display commemorates the three seamen from HMS *Petard* who boarded the stricken U-Boat U-559 and took off the vital codebooks needed to decipher Enigma traffic in the Battle of the Atlantic – two of them drowned as the submarine sank. There is a memorial to the three Polish mathematicians who cracked Enigma before the war and jump-started the Bletchley operation by sharing their knowledge with the British. An American garden, containing emblematic flora of the USA, celebrates the British–American intelligence co-operation that began at Bletchley Park with the arrival of a small party of US cryptanalysts in early summer 1943. The approach to Block B is dominated by a memorial to the veterans of Bletchley Park and its many outstations, emblazoned with re-arranged keyboard letters to say WE ALSO SERVED. The whole site is laid out in a way that insistently reminds us that the real stars are the thousands of ordinary men and women, service personnel and civilians, who worked here tirelessly to listen in on the enemy and win the war.

ROCHESTER – THE SPIRIT OF DICKENS

JEAN HAYNES

'Ah! Fine place – glorious pile – frowning walls – tottering arches – dark nooks – crumbling staircases – Old Cathedral too. Earthy smell – pilgrims' feet worn away the old steps – little Saxon doors – confessionals like money-takers' boxes at theatres. Queer customers, these monks – popes and Lord Treasurers and all sorts of old fellows with great red faces and broken noses, turning up every day – buff jerkins too – matchlocks – sarcophagus – fine place – old legends too – strange stories – capital!'

Who else could have written that but Charles Dickens? The famous author spent his formative years here, and later returned to the town to live and die, so making Rochester his own. Even today, two hundred years after his birth, the Dickens summer and Christmas festivals in the old city draw people in their thousands to see the places he knew and the characters he created. Costumed favourites – Fagin, Miss Havisham, Pickwick and Scrooge – roam its streets.

From Rochester station, turn right to the Star Hill crossing. Pause here and look up to your right. A portico, thrusting out over the pavement, indicates what was once the entrance to the Theatre Royal, run by the redoubtable Mrs Sarah Baker, who had theatres all round the Kent coast. Here young Dickens developed a lifelong passion for theatre.

Entering Rochester High Street, the visitor immediately notes the lines of ancient buildings. On the left, the timber-gabled house with grotesque carvings is described in *Great Expectations* as Mr Pumblechook's – the seed-merchant who takes young Pip to visit the mysterious Miss Havisham not far away in Crow Lane.

Stand at the gate of Restoration House, on the right, as Dickens did on the day before he died, and you will be looking at the old mansion where he imagined Miss Havisham lived: 'Of old brick and dismal. Some of the windows were walled up. There was a courtyard in front and that was barred, so we had to wait till someone should come to open it.' The pert Estella does so and explains that the house's name is 'Satis' for 'Enough'. In fact, the original Satis House, given that name by

Elizabeth I, who stayed there in 1573 as a guest of its owner, local MP Sir Richard Watts, stands at the other end of the town behind the castle.

At the time of Charles II's restoration, the owner of the house you are looking at had a special staircase built for the king's use and re-named his home 'Restoration House'. It is open to visitors in the summer, together with the recently discovered Tudor garden. Samuel Pepys, who was one of those escorting the king back to his realm, visited the neighbouring household and kissed the owner's wife in the cherry garden there. A later occupant named that house 'Pepys' Pleasure'.

Across the lane lies The Vines, a green shady park that once belonged to the monks of this cathedral city. The great storm of 1987 brought down many of its trees. A leisurely stroll takes you to the handsome buildings of the cathedral clergy, the Deanery, and the more modern ones of the King's School, which was founded in 1542.

Turn left into Minor Canon Row, home of Canon Crisparkle in *The Mystery of Edwin Drood*, the book Dickens was working on when he died. Seven of these fine houses have undergone restoration by the Spitalfields Trust. Actress Dame Sybil Thorndike, whose father was a minor canon and vicar of St Margaret's parish nearby, was born here. She was George Bernard Shaw's first 'St Joan'.

Dickens renamed the row Minor Canon Corner in his unfinished novel, and described it thus: '... a quiet place in the shadow of the Cathedral, which the cawing of the rooks, the echoing footsteps of rare passers, the sound of the Cathedral bell, the roll of the Cathedral organ seemed to render more quiet than absolute silence ... Red brick walls, harmoniously toned down in colour by time, strong-rooted ivy, latticed windows, panelled rooms, big oaken beams in little places and stone-walled gardens where annual fruit ripens upon monkish trees.'

On the right, you come to a secluded garden, part of the monastic lands, and to the left, the remains of the Bishop's Palace, where once John Fisher resided. He was executed, as was Sir Thomas More, because of matters surrounding Henry VIII's divorce from Catherine of Aragon, his first wife. Behind the garden lies Sir Richard Watts' Satis House.

Turn to the right again and you reach the front of the great cathedral. If the door is open, you will be able to share the view described by Dickens in *The Mystery of Edwin Drood*: 'In this lovely place in peace and quiet, a brilliant morning shines on the Old City. Its antiquities and ruins are surpassingly beautiful, with a lusty ivy gleaming in the sun and the rich trees waving in the balmy air. Changes of glorious light from the moving boughs, woods and fields or rather from the one great garden of the whole cultivated island in its yielding time, penetrate into the cathedral, subdue its earthy odour and preach the Resurrection and the Life. The cold tombs of centuries ago warm, and flecks of brightness dart into the sternest corners of the building, fluttering there like wings ... The great western folding door stood open on the fine bright, though short-lived, afternoon, for the airing of the place. In the free outer air the river, the green pastures and the brown arable lands, the teeming hills and dales were reddened by the sunset, while distant windows in windmills and farm homesteads, shone, patches of beaten gold.'

Flanking the cathedral is the great keep of the Norman castle. The green moat is where Dickens, in 1840, said he would like to be buried – 'There, my boy, I mean to go into dust and ashes' – but by 1870, when he died, it was closed for burials. There is a memorial to Dickens inside the cathedral, and a wreath is laid each June. However, to see the great man's last resting place you will have to go to Poet's Corner in Westminster Abbey.

Walk up the steep road to enter the castle's outer wall. Dickens described it thus in *The Pickwick Papers*: '... the ancient castle, its towers roofless, and its massive walls crumbling away, but telling us proudly of its own might and strength as when, seven hundred years ago, it rang with the clash of arms or resounded with the noise of revelry.'

When the Romans came to Britain, they came first to Rochester – Durobrivae they called it, 'the stronghold by the river' – where they built their earthworks. Centuries later, when the Normans arrived, they built on the Roman foundations. The round tower you see, at odds with its square companions, is the result of a fire that destroyed the original during a siege in 1215. Although now in ruins, a feeling of strength still emanates from the castle. Mr Pickwick again: 'I surveyed that massive ruin and thought what a brief little practical joke I seemed to be, in comparison with its solidarity, strength and length of life, and I went outside, and, standing in the solemn shadow of its walls, looking up at the blue sky, its only remaining roof ... I climbed the rugged staircase, stopping now and then to peep at the great holes where the rafters of its floors were once, bare and toothless now, or to enjoy glimpses of the Medway and, looking down at the old cathedral, the crumbling ruins of the old priory, the shrunken fragments of one of the city gates ... felt quite apologetic to the scene in general and for my own juvenility and insignificance.'

Mr Pickwick then descended to the bridge, and leant over the balustrades, 'contemplating nature and waiting for breakfast'. Should you wish to stay for a time in Rochester, there are some interesting old hostelries and good accommodation so that, on a fine morning, you may go for a pre-breakfast walk and lean on those same balustrades, moved now from the old bridge to the landscaped gardens of the Esplanade.

Today, the Esplanade in summer is bright with colourful flower-beds, and on the Medway beyond you can still see the sails of the yachts tacking westwards to the county town of Maidstone or eastwards towards Upnor. This little village, with its fine castle, was the scene of a near invasion when in 1667 the Dutch sailed up the Medway, fired some of the English fighting ships and broke the chain across the river. Samuel Pepys, Secretary to the Admiralty, was greatly relieved when the skirmish died down.

Turning to the right, past the little fourteenth-century Bridge House Chapel, you enter the High Street. Near the Crown pub, a plaque tells of a visit here by Henry VIII, incognito, in order to catch a glimpse of his future third wife, Anne of Cleves. Although he went through with the marriage, he hadn't liked what he'd seen and soon divorced her. Farther on, on the right, is the Royal Victoria and Bull. It used to be just The Bull, but when Princess Victoria sought accommodation here during a great storm, it got its regal name. The ballroom, reached by a fine staircase, still has the little gallery described by Dickens.

Opposite this old coaching inn is the Guildhall. Here Pip, in *Great Expectations*, came to be bound as an apprentice to Joe Gargery, the blacksmith: 'The Hall was a queer place, I thought, with higher pews than in church and with people hanging over the pews, looking on, and with the mighty justices (one in a powdered wig) leaning back in chairs, with folded arms, or taking snuff, or going to sleep, or writing or reading newspapers, and with some shiny black portraits on the walls which my inartistic eye regarded as a composition of hardbake and sticking-plaster. Here, in a corner, my indentures were duly signed and attested to and I was "bound". Mr. Pumblechook holding me all the while as if we had looked in on the way to the scaffold to have these little preliminaries attended to.'

The hall, the present council chamber of the town, is magnificent, and considered to be the finest seventeenth-century building in Kent. It was built in 1687 and is crowned by a weather vane of 1780 and a model of the ship *Rodney*. Here, surrounded by grand portraits under a beautiful plaster ceiling, the town's plate and chains of office are displayed. But the building houses more than this for it is also Rochester's museum. From the ground floor, the visitor moves through time from the prehistoric findings in the area to the dramatic events of its history – the Dutch raid and the Napoleonic wars when all the Medway towns were on constant alert for the invasion by Bonaparte. The crowning exhibition in this marvellous little museum is a representation of life on board a prisoner-of-war hulk. By the clever use of mirrors and sound effects, visitors can experience what it was like on the deck of an old dismasted warship, and descend into the orlop – the lowest deck – which would have been below the waterline, to see the depths to which prisoners were reduced.

Sir Cloudesley Shovell's is the famous name connected with the fine house that stands opposite the old Corn Exchange of 1698, which also bears his name. Caught in the great storm of 1703 off the Isles of Scilly, his ship was driven on to the shore and wrecked. He survived, but only long enough for a woman, scavenging among the wreckage, to find him unconscious and murder him for his great emerald ring.

The Corn Exchange, no longer a meeting place for merchants, has a vast Queen's Hall upstairs and a Prince's Hall on the ground floor, which is used for events and entertainments. Outside hangs a large town clock.

Dickens mentions the High Street often in his writings: 'Of course the town hall had shrunk fearfully since I was a child. I had entertained the impression that the High Street was at least as wide as Regent Street, London, or the Italian Boulevard at Paris. I found it little better than a lane. There was a public clock in it which I had supposed to be the finest clock in the world, whereas it turned out now to be as inexpressive, moonfaced and weak a clock as ever I saw … it is oddly garnished with a queer old clock which projects over the pavement from a grave red-brick building as if Time carried on business there and had hung out his sign.'

On the right, through Two Post Alley, you can catch a glimpse of the castle, while on the other side are the George Vaults, a crypt from the old monastic buildings. On the right-hand corner, the Kings Head Hotel, the Jolly Knight and Ye Arrow stand on a site where there has been an inn for the past four hundred years.

A surviving gatehouse from the monastery also stands on the right. Cemetery Gate and Chertseys Gate are two of its names, but it is perhaps better known as Jasper's Gate.

John Jasper is one of the main characters in *The Mystery of Edwin Drood*: '… and old stone gatehouse crossing the Close with an arched thoroughfare passing beneath it. Through its latticed windows a fire shines out upon the fast-darkening scene. A certain hush pervades the ancient pile, the cloisters and the churchyard after dark. One might fancy that the tide of life was stemmed by Mr Jasper's own gatehouse. The murmur of the tide is heard beyond, but no wave passes the archway over which his lamp burns red behind the curtain, as if the building were a lighthouse.'

Since Dickens did not live to finish the story, what became of Edwin remains a mystery, and whether or not his young uncle, the cathedral's choirmaster, is a villain. Jasper's lodging house was supervised by Mr Tope, the verger 'and showman, accustomed to be very high with excursion parties'.

A plaque on Lloyds Bank bears the name 'Abdication House'. It was from here that James II left for the Continent in 1688, marking the end of the Glorious Revolution and the start of the reign of Britain's only joint monarchs, William III and Mary II – strange that Rochester welcomed in one brother, Charles II, and saw the other out. Almost opposite the bank, on the right, Black Boy Alley was the scene of the murder in 1201 of a baker, who was struck down by his young assistant. Later, miracles that occurred in his name led to the baker being called St William of Perth, and this alley led to his shrine.

One of the most delightful houses in Rochester lies on the left, Sir Richard Watts' Six Poor Travellers House. In his will, the local MP and philanthropist left the wherewithal to provide a night's accommodation in this little building, plus a meal and fourpence, for six poor travellers at a time. This went on up until the Second World War. The building contains a number of small reception rooms and at the back, cell-like bedrooms. Beyond the building was a beautiful, tranquil walled garden. Dickens wrote of the place: 'I found it to be a clean, white house of a staid and venerable air, with a quaint old door (an arched door), choice little, long, low, latticed windows and a roof of three gables. Strictly speaking there were only six poor travellers but, being a traveller myself, though an idle one, and being withal as poor as I hope to be, I brought the number up to seven.'

In his story of the 'Seven Poor Travellers', Dickens treats the travellers to a fine meal, and now, every Christmas, a procession leaves from the Royal Victoria and Bull Hotel, acting out the story of the feast: 'Myself with the pitcher / Ben with the Beer / Inattentive boy with hot plates / Inattentive boy without hot plates / The TURKEY / Female carrying Sauces to be heated on the spot / The BEEF / Man with a heavy tray upon his head containing Vegetables and Sundries / Volunteer Hostler from the hotel grinning and rendering no assistance.'

Farther down the High Street you come to a square, surrounded by delightful dwellings, including La Providence, a retirement home for those of Huguenot descent. In the roadway nearby, just in front of where the nineteenth-century Sir Joseph Williamson's Mathematical School once stood (now relocated to Maidstone Road), the sites of the Roman earthworks and medieval walls are marked out by cobblestones. The large store on the right was the Travellers' Tuppeny, a less agreeable lodging than the Six Poor Travellers House.

At the end of the High Street stands Eastgate House, the finest of the half-timbered and brick buildings, dating back to 1590. It was built in the time of Sir Peter Buck, mayor of Rochester, and it has been many things since then, including a girls school. Dickens set *The Mystery of Edwin Drood* in the fictional town of Cloisterham, but it was a thinly disguised Rochester, and he tells us: 'In the midst of Cloisterham stands the Nuns' House, a venerable brick edifice, whose present appellation is doubtless derived from its conventional use. On the trim gate enclosing its courtyard is a resplendent brass plate, flashing forth the legend

"Seminary for the Young Ladies. Miss Twinkleton".'

Today this building is an atmospheric venue for entertainments, events and weddings. In the garden at the back stands Dickens' Swiss Chalet, which was sent to him by a friend, Fletcher, in ninety-four parts, and then erected in the grounds of his home, Gads Hill Place. The chalet was acquired by the Dickens Fellowship in 1961 and moved to its present site. The author used it as a retreat: 'I have put five mirrors in the chalet where I write and they reflect and refract in all kinds of ways, the leaves that are quivering at the window, and the great fields of corn, and the sail-dotted river. My room is among the branches of the trees and the birds and the butterflies fly in and out, and the green buds shoot in at the open windows, and the lights and the shadows of the clouds come and go with the rest of the company, and the scent of the flowers and, indeed, everything that is growing for miles and miles is most delicious.

'An ancient city, Cloisterham, and no meet dwelling-place for anyone with a hankering after the noisy world. A monotonous, silent city, deriving an earthy flavour from its Cathedral crypt and so abounding in vestiges of monastic graves, that the Cloisterham children grew small salad in the dust of abbot and abbesses and made dirt pieces of nuns and friars.'

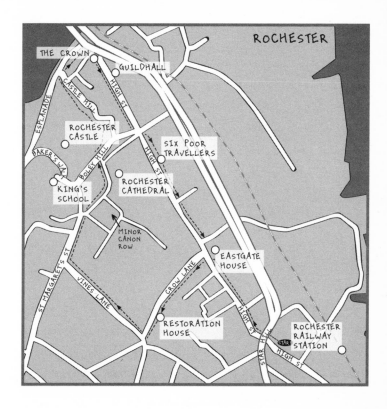

Come to Rochester today at Christmas and you will find a very different scene. Hundreds of visitors descend on the city to enjoy its traditional atmosphere and to revive the Dickensian spirit with which the immortal Boz endowed the festive season.

AUTHOR
BIOGRAPHIES

Richard Bartlett

was born and bred in London, and appeared on television, in films and on the stage for many years until London Walks approached him to create a theatre walk in Covent Garden. He never looked back and has been creating and guiding walks ever since. He conceived the idea of walks outside London in 1993/94 and now guides these day trips only. He splits his time between London and Suffolk in the summer and disappears to Cape Town for much of the winter.

John Blakey

eventually eschewed the glamour of mildewed theatre dressing rooms and freezing film sets – after an acting career spanning twenty-five years – in order to concentrate on writing and guiding. Based in London, during the summer months he is a professional Blue Badge driver-guide. He devotes the winter to writing. His first novel is nearing completion and he is developing original factual entertainment television projects for Side By Two Productions, which he runs with his wife. When not working, John likes running, and whizzing around London on his Vespa scooter, with his wife on the back, imagining that they're in the film *Roman Holiday*.

Gillian Chadwick

has been working as a Blue Badge guide in London and south-east England for nearly twenty years. Her career in the travel business spans over thirty years, during which time she has worked all over Europe, and further afield, as a tour director. She still enjoys showing groups the delights of her own country on British tours, and frequently visits Italy and France to maintain her linguistic skills and to learn even more about their food and culture. Gillian lives in West Sussex where she enjoys walking in the beautiful countryside, pottering in her garden and practising her cooking skills on friends and family.

Nick (Nicholas) Day

is an actor who has played a wide range of roles in theatre, television and film, and has recently been working with the Royal Shakespeare Company. Nick has appeared in some of the nation's most prestigious theatres, including the National Theatre, the Donmar, the Almeida and the Royal Court, and in the West End, and he has played guest roles in many television series, such as *Midsomer Murders*, *Doc Martin* and *Foyle's War*. He lives in Greenwich and it was his knowledge of, and love for, his home borough that led him to work for London Walks, when time allows.

Kim Dewdney

came to London from the 'frozen north' thirty years ago and immediately fell in love with the city. After spending seventeen years as a perpetual tourist, she decided to follow up her exploratory instincts professionally, trained for the London Blue Badge qualification and became a London Walks guide. Her enthusiasm has paid off as her husband, Rex, has now joined the London Walks team as well. Her daughter is an archaeologist and her son shares her love of football and Manchester United. Life could not be better and she looks forward to sharing many more gems – both in and out of London – with visitors.

Chris Green

is a classicist and a weaver, and a professionally qualified Blue Badge and City of London guide.

Jean Haynes

is a Londoner born and bred. She joined London Walks as a City of London guide after teaching for over thirty-five years, and conducts a wide range of tours, some in costume. As an actor, her leading roles have ranged from Greek drama and Shakespeare to music hall and pantomime. She lectures and writes on London, history, genealogy and literature, is a member of the Society of Genealogists and the Dickens Fellowship, and is on the committee of the Friends of Keats House.

Alison Hook

teaches part-time in a large comprehensive school in north-west London and was nominated by her students as teacher of the year, receiving second prize in the London finals. She holds many guiding qualifications – covering St Albans, the City of London and Docklands among other places – as well as the prestigious London Blue Badge. She received the accolade of being the best practical guide of her year on both the City and the Blue Badge course. Alison dedicates her chapter on

St Albans to her Uncle Gordon with whom she has explored the streets, buildings and museums of London. He supported and encouraged her through the Blue Badge course and is responsible for fostering her love of history.

Simon Law

was born in Windsor, Berkshire. He originally trained as a Blue Badge guide for the counties of Kent, Surrey and Sussex with the South-East of England Tourist Board, and subsequently gained more official regional accreditations, including for London, where he now mostly guides. He is one of just a few London Blue Badge guides privileged to hold the Cambridge Badge. Simon was a child chess champion. At his interview for Cambridge University he noted that he was the only candidate in the waiting room wearing a tie and the only one from a state school. He now avoids wearing ties and jeans. He has lived and worked on four continents, speaks several languages and has made numerous television appearances. He lives on the south coast.

Rex Osborn

came to London to study. He graduated in history from the London School of Economics, decided to stay and cannot imagine himself living anywhere else. He has been a public relations man, political campaigner, lobbyist and managing director of a firm in the City of London. He became a Blue Badge guide in 2010 (with more help than he cares to admit from a Blue Badge guide called Kim, his wife). Guiding fits in well with his work as an elected councillor in Tooting, South London.

Karen Pierce-Goulding

is a winner of the prestigious Blue Badge Guide of the Year Award and has been listed by *Travel & Leisure* magazine as one of the 'World's Greatest Tour Guides'. A journalist and reformed actress, Karen loves to tell a good story; her book *Royal London* was published in 2010. She and her husband, Adam, both regularly 'walk the streets' for London Walks. Karen dedicates her chapter to Adam and to their four-year-old daughter Isobella, who shares her daddy's boundless energy and enthusiasm for learning new things.

Hilary Ratcliffe

read history at Bristol University and taught in high schools before training as a City of London guide in 1991. She trained as a Blue Badge guide in 1998 and now works full-time as a tourist guide. She recently completed the St Albans city-guide course. In addition, Hilary is a Soroptimist, a member of the international business and professional women's service organisation, which works to improve the lot of women and girls worldwide. In her spare time she enjoys theatre, walking, reading and travelling.

David Tucker

broods over words, breeds enthusiasms and is 'unmanageable'. The seigneur of this favoured realm (London Walks), he's a balterer, literary historian, university lecturer and lifelong thanatophobe. He's also the London Walks 'pen' – he writes the famous white leaflet.

INDEX